WHO IS GOD?

by

REV. DR. FRANCES MCINTYRE

authorHOUSE™

1663 LIBERTY DRIVE, SUITE 200
BLOOMINGTON, INDIANA 47403
(800) 839-8640
WWW.AUTHORHOUSE.COM

© 2005 Rev. Dr. Frances Mcintyre All Rights Reserved.

No part of this book may be reproduced, stored in a retrieval system, or transmitted by any means without the written permission of the author.

First published by AuthorHouse 06/16/05

ISBN: 1-4208-5379-1 (sc)

Printed in the United States of America
Bloomington, Indiana

This book is printed on acid-free paper.

Dedication

Let it be known that God is in complete control of the writing of this book, which is the second book, which God, in His infinite wisdom, has caused me to write. On many occasions, it is and was God who gave me thoughts and words to include in the preparation, organizing, and information for the completion of this book. This book is published and dedicated to God and is written for the glory of God Almighty! I thank God for His wisdom, knowledge, understanding, guidance, love, and power as well as His grace, mercy, blessings, and protection. For God is great and greatly to be praised and His greatness is unsearchable. How marvelous and wondrous are His works. Praise God from whom all blessings flow. Whoever reads this book will be blessed because of the word of God, which is included in this book. It would be advantageous and helpful to everyone who will also read the first book which God gave me the wisdom, knowledge, and guidance to write, which is entitled "Love, Life, and Reality" and can be purchased from the internet at www.authorhouse.com or www.Amazon.com as well as Barnes and Nobles bookstores, or you may call: (773) 862-2755.

Table of Contents

Dedication v
Introduction 1
From the Author 3

Who Is God?

Meditations

- The Fruit of the Spirit 24
- Walk In the Spirit of God 29
- The Things We Cannot See 34
- I Love God Almighty, Jesus, and the Holy Spirit 39

Informational Observations

- Prisons, Penal Institutions and Law Enforcement ... 53
- Is It Wrong to Practice Homosexual, Lesbian, and Transvestite Activities? 58
- Success 63
- Time 67
- My Response and Observation to the article written by someone on the subject "Does the Church Have a Future?" 70
- My Response and Observation to an Article Written by Someone Regarding African-Americans: "Will Our Past Become Our Future?" . 73

Articles on Marriage…

- Neglected Wife 77
- Observations During a Traumatic Experience 80
- Trust 81
- Marriage Conflicts 83

Sermons
- What Is a Sermon? 93
- In The Beginning, God Created the Heaven and the Earth 97
- Eternal Life! 101
- Authority, Eternity, and Infinite 106
- Why and How Are We Created? 112
- God Is My Defense 118
- A Place Called Hell 123
- Power In The Word of God 131
- A Possible God In An Impossible Situation 136

Workshops
- How To Help Hurting People 140
- Faith and Stewardship Go Hand in Hand 149

PoemsAndPrayers
- The Sky 160
- Love 160
- A Prayer of Praise and Thanksgiving 162
- Prayer (6-14-2000) 165
- Prayer (10-01-2001) 167

Introduction

I thank God Almighty from whom all blessings flow. God is great and greatly to be praise and His greatness is unsearchable. For God is the beginning and the ending. God is the first and the last. Moreover, God is the source of all power. God is the source of all wisdom, knowledge, and understanding, and only God can give wisdom. It is the truth that only God can give wisdom, for without wisdom, we would not have the ability to learn and obtain knowledge nor would we have a sense of understanding because wisdom is knowledge guided by understanding. So, I truly thank God for the wisdom, knowledge, understanding, and strength, which He has given me to write a second book. This book is written and published for the glory of God. I have spent many hours night and day in order to complete this book, sometimes early in the morning and sometime late at night. I thank God for the perseverance that He has given to me. I pray that I will continue to use everything, which God has given to me, for His glory. Praise God for His excellent greatness, grace, goodness, and His mercy, which endures forever to all generations. I pray that God will continue to have complete control of this book, as well as the first book, including the publishing, distribution, marketing, and selling of the books. I also pray that God will bless everyone who reads this book. Some of you who read this book may wonder why I am redundant or repetitive in using the word "thanks". Ephesians 5:20 says: giving thanks always for all things unto God and the father in the name of our lord Jesus Christ. For God is most worthy of praise, obedience, service, and thanksgiving in that we obey and serve God only. Additionally, we must seek first the kingdom of God and His righteousness and all these other things will be added unto us. We must trust in the Lord with all our heart and lean not unto our own understanding, but in all our ways acknowledge God and He will direct our paths. Everyone who will take the time to read this book will be blessed because of the scriptural content (which is the word of God Almighty), which is contained in this book. Isaiah 55:10-11 says: For as the rain comes down and the snow from heaven, and returns not thither, but waters the earth, and makes it bring forth and bud, that it may give seed to the sower, and bread to the eater; so shall my word be that goes forth out of my mouth: it shall not return unto me void, but it shall accomplish that which I please, and it shall prosper in the thing whereto I sent it. In order for us as human beings to be right as well as successful, we must obey the word of God. Joshua 1:8 says: this book of the law shall not depart out of your mouth but you shall meditate therein day and night, that you may observe to do according to al that is written therein, for then you shall make your way prosperous and then you shall have good success. Praise God from whom all blessings flow.

From the Author

This book is written for the purpose of glorifying God. God, who is the most high God, for God is the beginning and the ending. It is the truth that God Almighty is the only one and true God. Isaiah 43:10 says: You are my witnesses says the Lord and my servant whom I have chosen: that you may know and believe me and understand that I am He: Before me there was no God formed neither shall there be after me. Revelation 1:8 says: I am Alpha and Omega, the beginning and the ending says the Lord, which is and which was, and which is to come, the Almighty. Romans 4:17 says: As it is written, I have made you a father of many nations before him whom he believed, even God, who quickens the dead and calls those things which be not as though they were. God is the source of all power! Romans 13:1 says: let every soul be subject unto the higher powers for there is no power but of God: the powers that be are ordained of God. Hebrews 4:12 says for the word of God is quick and powerful and sharper than any two-edged sword piercing even to the dividing asunder of the soul and spirit and the joints and marrow and is a discerner of the thoughts and intents of the heart. I thank and praise God for His wisdom, knowledge, courage, and understanding for it is and was God who gave me the ability and every thing, which is and was necessary for the writing and completion of this book. God's knowledge is infinite and inexhaustible for God knows everything and all things. And, God created all things. God is everywhere all the time and at the same time. God is all-powerful because it is the truth that God is the source of all power! Romans 4:13 says: let every soul be subject unto the higher powers for there is no power but of God: the powers that be are ordained of God! God is love and he loves us with an everlasting love. For from everlasting to everlasting, God is God. God is eternal. It is and was God who brought forth the verb "be". "Be" is an action word. It is a derivative of "I Am" for God is the great I Am, who, in the beginning said: Let there be light and there was light. So light came to be and began to exist because of the power of God (who is the beginning and ending and source of all power). God is and was before nothing. What is nothing? Nothing does not exist. God is from everlasting to everlasting. God is infinite and eternal. Praise God from whom all blessings flow.

Who

Is

GOD?

Who is God? God is the only creator. God is the beginning and the ending. God knows the ending at the beginning. God is the first and the last. Genesis 1:1 says: In the beginning God created the heaven and the earth! So, based upon this truth, it is evident that God is the beginning. God is the only true and living God for from everlasting to everlasting, God is God (Psalm 90:2 Isaiah 43:10). And, God will always be God. "Be" is the most used verb. In Genesis, the first chapter, verse three, we find these words: And God said let there be light and there was light! So, the truth of the matter is that light came to be or began to exist because of the power of God's word! God's word is quick and powerful and sharper than any two-edged sword, piercing even to the dividing asunder of the soul and spirit and of the joints and marrow, and is a discerner of the thoughts and intents of the heart (Hebrews 4:12). In other words, God, who created man and woman, can also separate the soul and spirit. God can also separate our joints. A joint is a part of a space included between the two joints of our bones. And only God can create and make a human body because it is and was God who created the human body in His own image and likeness. Genesis 1:26-27 says: And God said Let us make man in our image after our likeness and let them have dominion over the fish of the sea and over the fowls of the air and over the cattle and over all the earth and over every creeping thing that creeps upon the earth. So, God created man in His own image. In the image of God created He him, male and female created He them.

In today's times, scientists are in the process of cloning creatures, which they chose to call the personification or image of the person from which they used to clone the second person. The clone is exactly what they say it is – a clone. It is not a person or a human being because it is the indisputable truth that only God Almighty, the one and only Creator, can create. The truth of the matter is God made and created the scientist, who is trying to clone or make a duplicate of that which God has already created. Mankind or humans will never be able to make a person because they do not have the power nor the wisdom to do so. God and only God can create. Everything has already been created by God. In the gospel of John, which is the fourth book of the four gospels, John chapter one verses one through four: In the beginning was the Word and the Word was with God and the Word was God! The same was in the beginning with God! All things were made by Him and without Him was not anything made that was made. In Him was life and the life was the light of men! Man did not create or make himself. It is and was God Almighty, the Creator, who created man and woman. So, man cannot claim or name himself as author or maker of anything because the scientists had to have or use the things, which God had already created to make his or her invention. So, we do not have a valid claim or reason to do such things as trying to duplicate the things, which God has made already. We are not in the will of God, which means, we are out of order. God spoke everything into existence by the power of His word. And God said let there be light and there was light. Whatever God said "let there be…" came to be or began to exist based on the power of God's word! As it is written, I have made you a father of many nations before him whom he believed even God who quickens the dead and calls those things which be not as though they were!

God's power is infinite, endless, limitless, eternal, and reaches throughout eternity. For God is all-powerful. God transcends time and space. Because of God, we have time and space because God himself is time and space. Without God, there would be no time or space considering that we all live, move, and have our being in God because of His power and presence.

At this juncture, it is necessary to deal with or elaborate on causes and effects.

First of all, there has to be a cause before you can have an effect. For instance, when we go to the doctor, he inquires about our symptoms, and based on our symptoms, he or she can determine the nature of the illness. Thanks be unto God, who is the cause and the effect, because God Almighty caused the heavens and the earth to be and to exist. And, because God created the heavens and the earth by his omnipotent power, God is the cause and the effect. Without God, cause and effect could not exist or be. For God is the Creator and called everything into being or existence by the power of His word. God's word is living and has power. God is eternal. Isaiah 40:8 says: the grass withers, the flower fades: but the word of our God shall stand forever. Psalm 119:89 says: forever oh Lord your word is settled in heaven. God is all-powerful. Romans 13:1 says: let every soul be subject unto the higher powers for there is no power but of God: the powers that be are ordained of God. Psalm 33:6 says: by the word of the Lord were the heavens made and all the host of them by the breath of his mouth. Hebrews 11:3 says: through faith we understand that the worlds were framed by the word of God, so that things which are seen were not made of things which do appear.

God is synonymous to His word! God is His word! His word is God! In the book of John, the first chapter and the first verse, we find these words: In the beginning was the word, and the word was with God, and the word was God! God is the only source of all power for God is the beginning and the ending. Moreover, God knows the ending at the beginning. God is and was before nothing. What is nothing? Nothing does not exist. Based on Genesis, the first chapter, verse one: In the beginning God created the heaven and the earth! And, so, in this verse, we can clearly understand because of the wisdom of God, which God gave to us, that God is the only source of power, as well as being the source of everything! God is the "who?" because it is and was God who is and was the beginning. "What?" What was in the beginning? It is and was God which was in the beginning. "When?" When is the time of an event. God is the "when" because God is time. God transcends time and space. Without God, time and space would not exist because God himself is time and space. "Where?" means location or place. "In the beginning" because God is the beginning. "How?" How did God create the heaven and the earth? God created the heaven and the earth by the power of His word (Psalm 33:6, Hebrews 11:3). These scriptures are located on page 10 of this book. Did you know that the wind is one of God's treasures? Read Psalm 135:7. God does and can cause the wind to move and do whatever he wants it to do. God made the wind, and the wind belongs to God. The wind obeys God. God can speak to the wind, and the wind will become strong or calm. The sea obeys God. The devil and his demons obey God! Everything obeys God because God is in complete control of everything and all things, whether they are visible or invisible! You may ask what are some of the things which are invisible? The wind is invisible. The mind is invisible. Our voice is invisible. Angels are sometimes invisible. And, it is God Almighty who created all these things and more. The truth of the matter is: it is and was God who created and made everything!

God is everywhere all the time at the same time. He never slumbers or sleeps. Psalm 121:4 (Please read.) God's eyes are in every place looking at the evil and the good (Proverbs 15:3). God knows our thoughts even before they come into our minds (Psalm 139:1-18; Hebrews 4:12-13). God made the day and He also made the night. God is the past. God is today. God is the future. Without him, there would be no past, no today, no future. Because of God, we had the past; we have today; and we have the future. God made the water, which is beautiful, pure, and crystal clear. Scientists claim or speculate that the world spins or rotates on an axis. But, listen to this! The truth of the matter is that the earth is supported by the power of God Almighty! Ecclesiastes 3:11-15 says: He has made every thing beautiful in His time: also He has set the world in their heart so that no man can find out the work that God made from the beginning to the end. I know that there is no good in them, but for man to rejoice and to do good in his life. And, also that every man should eat and drink and enjoy the good of all his labor. It is the gift of God! I know that whatever God does it shall be forever! Nothing can be put to it nor anything taken from it. And, God does it that men should fear before him. That which has been is now, and that which is to be has already been; and God requires that which is pass. Hebrews 11:3 says: through faith we understand that the worlds were framed by the word of God, so that things which are seen were not made of things which do appear.

God is great! And, God so majestically made the lofty mountains and deep valleys, covered with green grass like a lovely blanket. God made the sky so high that it cannot be touched by humanity. The blueness of the sky is magnificent, created by the almighty power of God. God is the origin and the only source of power. God is the past. God is today. God is the future. Because of God, the past did exist, and because of God, we have today, and the future and life forever more. For God so loved the world that He gave his only begotten son that whosoever believes in Him shall not perish but have everlasting life! God walks upon the wings of the wind and makes the clouds his chariot. God walks on the raging sea. God speaks to the sea, and the sea becomes calm and still. Everything must obey the will of God; demons or whatever it be, they all shall obey the will of God! Because God is in complete control of everything and all things! God controls even things that are invisible. Colossians 1:16-17 says: For by Him were all things created, that are in heaven and that are in earth, visible and invisible, whether they be thrones or dominions or principalities or powers: all things were created by Him and for Him. And, He is before all things and by Him all things consist. Isaiah 43:10 says: You are my witnesses said the Lord, and my servant, whom I have chosen: that you may know, and believe me and understand that I am He before me there was no God formed, neither shall there be after me. God is the beginning and the ending. God knows the ending even at the beginning. God knows what is going to happen even before it happens or occurs. God can see the day and the night even before they come into existence because it is God who made the day and the night. Genesis 1:3-5 says: And God said let there be light and there was light, and God saw the light that it was good and God divided the light from the darkness. And God called the light day and the darkness He called night, and the evening and the morning were the first day. And, so, by the power of God's word, light and darkness, the day and night, came to be and began to exist. Read Genesis, chapters one and two. These two chapters inform or tell us about all the things which God created and made. God is love, life, mercy, grace, goodness, infinite, eternity, the Creator, and the maker of everything! Because God is and was before nothing. What is nothing? Nothing does not exist. The truth of the matter is that God is the only source of power! Romans 13:1 says: let every soul be subject unto the higher powers. For there is no power but of God: the powers that be are ordained of God. All power belongs to God Almighty. God is great, and His greatness is unsearchable! God's great mercy endures forever to all generations. Morning by morning, new mercies we see and all that we have needed, God has already provided. Great is the Lord's mercy unto all of us. Thank you God for your many gifts, which are innumerable because of the magnitude. Thank you God for your great wonderful and eternal salvation through your son Jesus Christ who is our Lord and Savior. Thank you God for your many, many blessings, which you bestow upon us daily. Lord, we love you. We adore you. We praise you for your excellent greatness and for your miraculous miracles. For your ways are past man's finding out and above mankind's comprehension. Isaiah 55:8-9 says: for my thoughts are not your thought; neither are your ways my ways says the Lord. For as the heavens are higher than the earth, so are my ways higher than your ways and my thoughts than your thoughts. God is our light and our salvation, and because God is our life, light, and our salvation, we have nothing to fear or be afraid of. God is always there to protect us. God never slumbers or sleeps (Psalm 121:4). His eyes are in every place looking at the good and the evil (Proverbs 15:3). We are not able to do anything without the help of God! God is independent, but we are dependent on God for all things and everything! We cannot inhale or exhale without the power of God, nor can we awake from sleep without the power of God. It is and was God who caused us to awake after we have been asleep. It is not by accident, nor did the alarm clock awaken us. The truth of the matter is only God knows the procedure for going to sleep, and He also causes us to awake. God is great and His greatness is unsearchable! God walks upon the wings of the wind, and He makes the clouds His chariots. God sends the lightnings, and the lightnings go. The lightnings respond to God by saying: "Here we are" (Job 38:35). God sends the rain and snow from heaven to water the earth (Isaiah 55:10). God makes a way in the sea and a path in the mighty waters. God walks upon the sea. The power of God caused Jesus and Peter to walk on the sea (Matthew 14:25-29). Jesus, by the power of God, spoke to the wind and said: "Peace. Be still.", and the wind ceased and became calm, and the waves of the sea became calm and still. Everything obeys the voice and will of God, demons or whatever it be, they all shall obey the voice and power of god. God makes a way in the wilderness and rivers in the desert (Isaiah 4:19). Thus says the Lord your redeemer and H that formed you from the womb, I am the Lord that makes all things that stretch forth the heavens alone that spreads abroad the earth by myself (Isaiah 44:24). Before we call God, He will answer and while we are yet speaking, He will hear. Isaiah 65:24 The Lord said call unto me and I will answer you and show you great and mighty things, which you do not know (Jeremiah 33:3). For with God all things are possible (Matthew 19:26). God is the past. God is today. God is the future. Without God, there would not be the past, nor today, nor would there be the future. But, because of God, we had the past, and we have today and the future: because God is all three. Because God is the beginning and the ending! God is the first and the last for from everlasting to everlasting, God is God! Moreover, God will always be God! God is the source of all power and it is the truth, the only truth that it is and was God who created and made everything and all things; things that are visible and things that are invisible. Colossians 1:16 says for by Him were all things created that are in heaven and that are in the earth, visible and invisible, whether they be thrones or dominions or principalities or powers. All things were created by Him and for Him.

The Lord is our living place. We move, live, and have our being in God! And, because of God! We are or we "be", only because of God! God is the great I Am! I Am existed before "be" because I Am said in the beginning of creation: and God said let there be light and there was light! And, because of the power of God's word, light came to be and began to exist and will always be or exist. Because God is light and God is eternal and forever. God is before all things and by Him all things consist. Revelation 21:23 says: and the city had no need of the moon to shine in it for the glory of God did lighten it and the lamb is the light thereof. We must all know God in a personal way. How do we get to know God?

1. We must hear and read the word of God, which is found in the Holy Bible, which was written by holy men chosen by God to write his holy word, as they were guided by the Holy Spirit of God. We must not try to interpret the word of God nor listen to others who try to interpret the word of God. II Peter 1:20-21 says: knowing this first, that no prophecy of the scripture is of any private interpretation for the prophecy came not in old time by the will of man: but holy men of God spoke as they were moved by the Holy Spirit. And, so, we must rely on the Holy Spirit to interpret and guide us as we read and share the word of God with others. Whether it is in teaching, preaching, or witnessing, we must ask God to let His Holy Spirit guide and teach us as we share God's word with others. We must diligently and faithfully study the word of God daily as we are guided by the Holy Spirit of God. We must be knowledgeable about the word of God and know God and His word. It is very necessary that we understand the word of God because when we know God and His word and walk and live our lives according to the word and will of God, we will be effective in sharing the word of God with others as we witness to them from the Holy Word of God as we are guided by the Holy Spirit of God. We must know Jesus Christ, the Son of God, for it was Jesus Christ who died for our sins on the cross of Calvary. Jesus died an agonizing, shameful, and painful death for the sins of the whole

world. They beat, mocked, and even spit on him, but Jesus did not complain. He willingly gave his sinless, perfect life for all of us so that we can and will live forever in the kingdom of God, Christ, and the Holy Spirit. Jesus shed his precious blood on Golgotha to save us, and his blood will never lose its power! It reaches to the highest mountain, and it flows to the lowest valley. We must first hear and believe and understand the word of God.

2. We must believe that Jesus Christ is the Son of God Almighty and that He died for our sins but He rose again on the third day with all power in heaven and in the earth in His hands, given to Him by God, the Father.

3. We must ask God to forgive us for our sins and we must accept Jesus Christ as our Lord and Savior in that we obey Him and follow His example, for Jesus is the one and only role model which we all must follow, in order to live a righteous life before God and humanity. We do not have an option. It is very necessary that we know Jesus Christ as our personal Lord and Savior, and we must know the word of God, which gives us directions regarding the lifestyle of Jesus.

We must live a holy and righteous life as we follow the example of Jesus. The scripture says: Be you holy for I am holy (I Peter 1:16). I Peter 1:15 says: but as He, which has called you is holy, so be you holy in all manner of conversation. This can be done when we know God and His word. We must also obey God and His word, as well as be faithful in reading the word of God daily. Also, we must pray daily unto God for guidance, wisdom, knowledge, and understanding regarding the word of God and His instructions. When we know and follow the word of God, we will do what is right according to His word. It is essential that we have a daily diet of the word of God. Matthew 4:4 says: But He answered and said it is written man shall not live by bread alone but by every word that proceeds out of the mouth of God. As I reiterate, we must have a daily diet of the word of God and live by it. When we live according to the word of God, we will be healthy spiritually, mentally, and physically. Colossians 2:10 says: and you are complete in Him which is the head of all principalities and power! But thanks be unto God who gives the victory through our Lord and Savior, Jesus Christ (I Corinthians 15:57). It is most important to know that God is omnipotent, which means that He is all-powerful. God is omnipresent, which is defined as: God is everywhere all the time at the same time. God is omniscient, which is defined as: God knows everything. And, rightly so, because it is and was God who created everything and all things. Isaiah 44:24 says: thus said the Lord your redeemer and He that formed you from the womb, I am the Lord that makes all things that stretched forth the heavens alone, that spread abroad the earth by myself. In the beginning was the word, and the word was with God and the word was God. The same was in the beginning with God. All things were made by Him, and without him was not anything made that was made. In Him was life and the life was the light of men. And, the light shone in darkness and the darkness did not understand the light. God is love. God is grace, mercy, power, excellent, infinite, eternal, eternity. God is forever and more, for from everlasting to everlasting, God is God and God has always existed, and He lives forever more! God is the first and the last! God is the beginning and the ending! God knows the ending at the beginning! God has seen wisdom because God, himself, is wisdom! Wisdom comes from God. Only God can give wisdom. Wisdom is very necessary because without wisdom, we would not have understanding. Wisdom gives us the ability to understand things. Without wisdom from God, we would be void of understanding. Nor would we be able to learn anything. But, thanks be unto God who gives us wisdom liberally. We have so much for which we must and should give thanks unto God Almighty for His many bountiful blessings, which are innumerable for we cannot count them numerically because of the multitude. God is great and He is greatly to be praised, and His greatness in unsearchable. God is wonderful. How marvelous are His works. God's power heals all manner of sickness and diseases. God can speak and a man will lay down and die. He can speak again, and that same man will get up and live again. Praise God from whom all blessings flow. Thank God for His unsearchable riches, which he gives to all of us. Everything that we have comes from God. We have not earned anything because everything belongs to God. Psalm 24 says: the earth is the Lord's and everything in the earth belongs to God, the world and they that live in the world. For it is God who made the heavens and the earth and everything in the heavens and everything in the earth. The truth of the matter is God made everything, things that are visible and things that are invisible! God is most worthy of all praise and thanksgiving! God loves us with an everlasting love! God is the most high God! Psalm 92:1 says: It is a good thing to give thanks unto the Lord and to sing praises unto your name oh most high. Psalm

92:8 says: but you Lord are most high forevermore! Psalm 91:1 says: He that lives in the secret place of the most high shall abide under the shadow of the Almighty! God is the creator and the maker of all things. We must obey God only, and we must serve God only! We must praise and thank God everyday! – in the morning, at noon day, at evening time, and during the night, for God is most worthy of all praise and thanksgiving! For God created us for His glory (Isaiah 43:7). We must love the Lord our God with all our heart, with all our soul, with all our mind, and with all our strength and love our neighbor as ourselves. We must seek first the kingdom of god and His righteousness and all these things shall be added unto us. We must trust in the Lord with all our heart and lean not upon our own understanding but in all our ways acknowledge God and He will direct our path. We must keep our minds stayed on the Lord for when we concentrate on God, He will keep us in perfect peace because we trust in Him. Trust in the Lord Jehovah forever for in the Lord Jehovah is everlasting strength! The goodness, mercy, grace, blessings, power, and love of God is forever and cannot be measured, and is inexhaustible. Let it be known that it is God Almighty the Creator who is in complete control of the writing of this book. I, myself, cannot do anything without the power of God to guide and strengthen me. And, I am totally dependent on God for wisdom, knowledge, and understanding for the writing of this book. This book is written for the glory of God! I have been awakened by God late at night and sometimes early in the morning in order to write the things which God would have me to include in this book. I pray that God will help me to obey Him completely as I pen this book according to His will. I also ask that the Holy Spirit will guide me every step of the way regarding the writing of this book in Jesus' name. Amen. The Holy Bible, which contains the word of God, begins with God, and it also ends with God. It is the first historical book written and from this book, all other history books were derived. Without the Holy Bible, which is the Holy Word of God Almighty, there could not be nor would there be any other history books such as early world history, Oriental History, African History, European History, Egyptology, Occidental, etc. Genesis 1:1 and Revelation 22:21 is written and is living proof that the Bible, which is the living word of God and the Truth (the ONLY truth), as well as being the infallible and inerrant word of God!

Let's take a closer look at Genesis 1:1, which is the very first verse recorded in the Bible, which is God's Holy Word! This is a truly profound verse because it begins with God!! And, we know, based on the Bible, that God truly is the beginning and the ending and is the first and the last. God is and was before nothing. What is nothing? Nothing does not exist. "Is" is a derivative of "be". "Be" is defined as you exist, live, or have your being. I Am is God, and God, in the beginning, said let there be light and there was light! And, so, because of the word of God, light came to be and began to exist. Because of the power of God's word and the great I Am, who is God, called everything into being or into existence. It is the truth that whatever God said let there be came to be because of God's word! And, so, the great I Am brought forth the verb "be", which is an action word spoken by God Almighty, which came forth from God and is God. God's Holy Word is living and has power. God's word is eternal. God is His word. His Word is Him. In other words, God is synonymous to His word.

Words are very important. We must be very careful how we use words because words can encourage or can be injurious, or they can hurt others. And, so, let us use words that will encourage and be helpful to others. There are many more adjectives and adverbs, which are descriptive of God, but mere words cannot adequately describe who God is. But, we know because of the word of God, that God lives forever! He is infinite, eternal – He is life! He is the only Creator. He is the only source of all power! For He alone is all-powerful. He knows everything and all things! Because it is and was God who created everything in the heavens and in the earth, things that are visible and those things that are invisible. They were and are created by the omnipotent power of God Almighty. God is the great I Am. I Am is defined as being self-existent, which applies only in reference to God. God referred to Himself as I Am when He told Moses to go down into Egypt and tell Pharaoh to let His people, the children of Israel, go free out of the land of Egypt. Moses asked God who shall I say sent me? And God said unto Moses: I Am that I Am. And, He said thus shall you say unto the children of Israel: I Am has sent me unto you! I can go on an on talking about the wonderful, beautiful, lovely and great things about God. There are so many wonderful things about Him. His name is wonderful. He is a mighty good counselor! He is the mighty God, the everlasting Father! He is the prince of peace! He is a healer who heals all manner of sickness and all manner of diseases. God looks down upon the earth from heaven and He can see everywhere, and He can see everything because God is everywhere all the time at the same time! Nothing is too hard for God! God specializes in doing things that are impossible. For with God, all things are possible! Matthew

19:26 – But Jesus beheld them and said unto them, with men this is impossible, but with God all things are possible!

God is great and greatly to be praised, and His greatness is unsearchable. We must praise God, and we must give humble thanks unto God for who He is! For God is the source of all power! And, He is the source of all blessings! We cannot do anything without the power and help of God! Thanks be unto God for His unspeakable gifts which He bestows upon us daily, moment by moment. Time would not permit me to exhaust, nor can words fully or completely express the identity and personality of God. Hebrews 1:2 says: has in these last days spoken unto us by His son whom He has appointed heir of all things, by whom also He made the worlds, who, being the brightness of His glory and the express image of His person. And, upholding all things by the word of His power, when He had, by Himself, purged our sins, sat down on the right hand of the majesty on High. These verses will help us to understand who God is and how wonderful He is, as well as all of the verses in the word of God, help us to understand that God is in complete control of everything and all things! The Holy Word of God helps us to realize that because of God, we exist, move, live, and have our being. Also, because of God, everything is and does exist because of God's power. Hopefully, the things that God has helped and allowed me to share with each person or persons who read(s) this book will know and understand more about who God is. I also pray that God will be and continue to be in complete control of the publishing, distribution, selling, and marketing of this book. And, I pray that God will bless all who will take the time to read this book. Praise God from whom all blessings flow!

Meditations

The Fruit of the Spirit

Thanking God from whom all blessings flow. I greet you in the name of Jesus Christ, the Son of God, and the Holy Spirit, the comforter, which is the working power of God. God Almighty is the beginning and the ending, for God knows the ending at the beginning. Moreover, God is the first and the last because God is the source of all power! God is and was before nothing. What is nothing? Nothing does not exist. For from everlasting to everlasting, God is God. And, God will always be God.

The subject of this message is the fruit of the spirit. The scriptural text is found in Galatians, the fifth chapter, verses 22 and 23 as well as other supporting scriptures found in the Holy Bible, namely Ephesians, chapter five verse nine; Philippians chapter one, verse eleven; and Romans, the eighth chapter, verse twenty-three.

Perhaps, at this juncture, we need to know and identify who the Holy Spirit is. The Holy Spirit is the third person in the godhead, which is the working power of God Almighty! The Holy Spirit was with God in the beginning, according to Genesis chapter one, verse two, which says: and the earth was without form, and void, and darkness was upon the face of the deep, and the spirit of God moved upon the face of the waters. Jesus Christ was also in the beginning with God. Genesis 1:26 says: and God said, let us make man in our image after our likeness: and let them have dominion over the fish of the sea and over the fowl of the air, and over the cattle and over all the earth, and over every creeping thing that creeps upon the earth. The plural pronoun is indicative of more than one, which is and was God, Jesus, and the Holy Spirit. God is the first person in the Godhead. Jesus said in John 17:5: and now O Father, glorify me with your own self with the glory, which I had with you before the world was. God is and was first because God is the beginning and the ending. God is the first and the last. God is the Alpha and the Omega. For from everlasting to everlasting, God is God. Because God knows the ending at the beginning. Isaiah 43:10 says: you are my witnesses said the Lord and my servants whom I have chosen that you may believe me and understand that I am He; before me, there was no god formed, neither shall there be after me! God is and was before nothing. What is nothing? Nothing does not exist. You can have a million zeroes, and they still equal nothing. One plus one is two, but zero plus zero is still zero.

God is the source of all power! Romans 13:1 says: let every soul be subject unto the higher powers for there is no power but of God: the powers that be are ordained of God. For the word of God is quick and powerful and sharper than any two-edged sword, penetrating even to the dividing asunder of soul and spirit and of the joints and marrow and is a discerner of the thoughts and intents of the heart. Just think about that for a moment ... God knows our thoughts even before they come into our minds.

Jesus Christ is the second person in the Godhead. Some people or theologians use the word "trinity", but trinity is not in the Holy Bible. Colossians 2:9.10 & 12 says: for in Him lives all the fullness of the Godhead bodily. And, you are complete in Him, which is the head of all principality and power. Buried with Him in baptism, wherein also you are risen with him through the faith of the operation of God who has raised him from the dead. And, the Holy Spirit, who is the comforter, is the third person in the Godhead.

What are the fruit of the spirit? Love – because God is love. I John 4:8 says: he that does not love does not know God for God is love. There is no fear in love but perfect love casts out fear: because fear has torment. He that fears is not made perfect in love. II Timothy 1:7 says: for God has not given us that spirit of fear but of power, love and a sound mind. Joy – for the kingdom of God is not meat and drink but righteousness, peace, and joy in the Holy Spirit. Peace – we who are Christians have the peace of God, which passes all understanding, which shall keep our hearts and minds through Christ Jesus. Longsuffering – we are children of God and heirs of God and joint heirs with Christ. If so be that we suffer with Him that we may be also glorified together. Gentleness – as Christians, we must not speak evil of others. We must not be brawlers or troublemakers. But we must be gentle, showing all meekness unto all men. Goodness – surely goodness and mercy shall follow me all the days of my life and I will live in the house of God forever (Titus 3:2, Psalm 23:6). Faith – great is the Lord's faithfulness and His compassion does not fail because morning by morning, new mercies we see, and all that we have needed, God has provided. Great is the Lord's faithfulness. Meekness – Matthew 5:5 says blessed are the meek for they shall inherit the earth. Temperance – we must be controlled completely by the Holy Spirit of God as were Daniel, Shadrach, Meshach, and Abedneggo. They refused to eat the king's meat and they chose to obey God instead of Nebuchadnezzar. We must walk in the power of the Holy Spirit of God, and we will not fulfill the lust of the flesh. God has given us instructions and the formula for walking in the Spirit.

1. We must know God and His word.

2. It is essential that we also obey God and His word so that we will know what and how to do what God is telling us to do. (We must also know the things which we must NOT do according to the instructions found in God's Holy Word.)

As born again Christians, those of us who have heard and read the word of God and have believed that Jesus Christ is the Son of God and that He died for our sins and we have accepted Jesus Christ as our Lord and savior and asked God to forgive us for our sins, we have eternal life through our Lord and Savior Jesus Christ. There is therefore now no condemnation to them which are in Christ Jesus, who walk not after the flesh but after the Spirit. For the law of the Spirit has made me free from the law of sin and death. For what the law could not do in that it was weak through the flesh, God, sending His own son in the likeness of sinful flesh and for sin, condemned sin in the flesh that the righteousness of the law might be fulfilled in us who walk not after the flesh but after the Spirit. For they that are after the flesh do mind the things of the flesh but they that are after the Spirit, the things of the Spirit. For to be carnally minded is death; but to be spiritually minded is life and peace. Because the carnal mind is enmity against God. For it is not subject to the law of God; neither indeed can be. So, then, they that are in the flesh cannot please God. If we practice what Philippians 4:8 tells us to do, we will not sin. Philippians 4:8 says: Finally, brothers, whatsoever things that are true, whatsoever things that are honest, whatsoever things that are just, whatsoever things that are pure, whatsoever things that are lovely, whatsoever things that are of a good report; if there be any virtue and if there be any praise, think on these things. And, if you have a problem, move to the 13th verse, which says: I can do all things through Christ who strengthens me. And, if you still have a problem, move to the 19th verse, which says: but my God shall supply all YOUR needs according to His riches in glory by Christ Jesus. Now unto God and our Father, be glory forever and ever. Amen.

Galatians 5:16 says: This I say then. Walk in the spirit and you will not fulfill the lust of the flesh. Rejoice in the Lord always and again I say rejoice. This can be done when we know God and His word. We must also obey God and His word. God will surely help us to obey Him and His word. And, again, I say: Walk in the Spirit of God and you will not sin or fulfill the lust of the flesh. Walk on by faith in God. Praise and thank God from whom all blessings flow.

Walk In the Spirit of God

Praise God from whom all blessings flow. The scriptural text for this message is found in the letter of Paul to the Romans, the eighth chapter, verses 1-17. This letter was written after the conversion of Paul. Paul, in his introduction, makes it very clear that he was called to be a servant and an apostle of Jesus Christ, to preach the gospel of God. He greeted the saints of Rome very warmly by the grace and peace of God. The subject of this message is: Walk in the Spirit of God!

I believe, at this juncture, we need to know who the Holy Spirit is. The Holy Spirit is the working power of God!!! He is also the third person in the Godhead. Colossians 2:9-10 – the three persons in the Godhead are God Almighty, the Creator, Jesus Christ, who is the only begotten son of God, and the Holy Spirit, who is the Comforter. God is the source of all power! The truth of the matter is that God is the beginning and the ending. God is the first and the last. God is the Alpha and Omega. God is the cause and the effect. It is a scientific fact that before there can be an effect, there must be a cause! For an example, there is a cause for an illness or sickness. A doctor can determine the cause of an illness based on the symptoms. There is a cause for a divorce. Something had to have happened or occurred which precipitated the event or effect. But, listen to this! God is the cause and the effect! Because God is the beginning and the ending. God is the first and the last. As a matter of truth, God is and was before nothing. What is nothing? Nothing does not exist. God has always existed. God is the past. God is the present. And, God is the future. For from everlasting to everlasting, God is

God! Before God Almighty, the Creator, there was no god formed, neither shall there be after because God is the only true and eternal God. Because God is the beginning and the ending. God is the first and the last. Moreover, God is the beginning and source of all power! There is no god beside Him.

"Be" is the most used verb in the English language because God used the action verb "be" to create. During the time of creation, God said let there be light, and there was light! And, so, based on the power of God's word, light came to be and began to exist. "Be" is a derivative of I Am, which is a title God used when He told Moses to go to Egypt and tell Pharaoh to let His people go from Egypt to the land of Canaan. God told Moses to tell them I Am that I Am has sent you. And, this title means "self-existence". We, as human beings, created by God, are not independent. But, we are totally dependent on God to sustain or to take care of us. For we move, live, and have our being in God. And, because of God, we be and do exist or live because of God's power!

And, so, as Christians, we have the power of God, which is the Holy Spirit, to keep us and teach us as well as guide and comfort us. And, we praise and thank God for His Holy Spirit. But, we must walk in the Spirit! Because when we walk in the Spirit of God, we will not sin. And, we will not fulfill the lust of the flesh. Romans 8:1-2 says: There is therefore now no condemnation to them, which are in Christ Jesus, who walk not after the flesh, but after the Spirit. Fro the law of the spirit of life in Christ Jesus has made me free from the law of sin and death. Fro what the law could not do, in that it was weak through the flesh, God, sending His own son in the likeness of sinful flesh, and, for sin, condemned sin in the flesh, that the righteousness of the law might be fulfilled in us, who walk not after the flesh but after the Spirit. And, so… There is therefore now no condemnation to them, which are in Christ Jesus, who walk not after the flesh, but after the Spirit. Galatians 5:16 says: This I say then, walk in the Spirit, and you will not fulfill the lust of the flesh. Because the flesh lusts against the Spirit and the Spirit against the flesh, and these are contrary the one to the other: so that you cannot do the things that you should. But, if we are led of the Spirit, we will not fulfill the lust of the flesh.

It is impossible to sin when we follow completely the guidance and teaching of the Holy Spirit. We must follow as the Holy Spirit leads us so that we can live a righteous life according to the Word and according to the will of God our heavenly father. God has given us instructions and the formula regarding how to walk in the Spirit.

1. We must yield and submit ourselves completely unto the will of God and be guided by the Holy Spirit and we will not fulfill the lust of the flesh. Because God has not given us the spirit of fear but of power, love, and a sound mind.

2. We must not allow our hearts or minds to be troubled.

3. We must trust in the Lord with all of our heart and not lean unto our own understanding but in all your ways acknowledge God and He will direct our paths.

4. We must seek first the kingdom of God and His righteousness and all these other things will be added unto us.

5. We must pray and read the word of God before we begin our daily activities. Prayer and the reading of God's word must be the first thing on our daily agenda.

6. Whatever we do, in word or deed, it must be done for the glory of God. Our thoughts must be righteous. WE must do what Philippians 4:8 says: Finally, brothers, whatsoever things that are true, whatsoever things that are honest, whatsoever things that are just, whatsoever things that are pure, whatsoever things that are lovely, whatsoever things that are of good report; if there be any virtue and if there be any praise, think on these things. And, this can be done because Philippians 4:13 & 19 says: I can do all things through Christ who strengthens me. But my God shall supply all your needs according to His riches in glory by Christ Jesus.

7. We must know God and His word, and we must obey God and His word as we are guided by the Holy Spirit. We must also know Jesus Christ as our Lord and Savior, and we must follow His example and lifestyle. We must also thank God for His many blessings and gifts, which he gives to us daily, moment by moment.

We have life and blessings because of God's love and mercy. And, in my conclusion, I leave these words with you from Romans 8:35-39: who shall separate us from the love of Christ? Shall tribulation or distress or persecution or famine or nakedness or peril or sword? As it is written, for your sake, we are killed all the day long. We are accounted as sheep for the slaughter. No, in all these things, we are more than conquerors through Him that loved us. For I am persuaded that neither death nor life, nor angels, nor principalities, nor powers, nor things present, nor things to come, nor height, nor depth, nor any other creature shall be able to separate us from the love of God, which is in Christ Jesus our Lord. Walk in the Spirit and you will not fulfill the lust of the flesh. Praise God from whom all blessings flow.

The Things We Cannot See

There are things which we cannot see, things that are invisible. What are some of the things that are invisible? The mind is invisible, but nevertheless, the mind does exist, and it is a vital entity or part of our being. Moreover, it is functional and a very important part of our body. For without the mind, our body could not function properly for the mind is our reasoning faculty, which causes or gives us the ability to think and do things that are necessary for our survival.

Wisdom is also something that we as human being cannot see, but God can see wisdom for God himself is wisdom! (Job 28:1-28) And, so, wisdom comes from God and only God can give us true wisdom. James 1:5 says: if any of you lack wisdom, let him ask of God that gives to all men liberally and upbraids not and it shall be given him. Wisdom is knowledge, guided by understanding, and only God can give true wisdom. Without the wisdom of God, we would not have the ability to learn or to obtain knowledge and understanding. For without the wisdom of God, we would be dysfunctional and void of understanding. It is the truth that without the wisdom of God, it would be impossible to perform our daily activities. But, with God, all things are possible. Matthew 19:26 says: But Jesus looked at them and said unto them: with men this is impossible, but with God all things are possible.

Thoughts are invisible, but when we have an idea, which is a mental image or thought, we can express the idea or thought in written words or we can express it in inventions. We must remember that it is God who gives us the wisdom and power to do all the things, which we are able to do. For without God, it is impossible for us to perform or do anything regardless of what it is that we intend to do. We cannot do it without the wisdom and power of God Almighty because we are and must be dependent on God for all things. But, God is independent. God can do anything that He wants to do. He can do whatever He wants to do and when and how He will do it. Because God is the beginning and the ending. God is the first and the last. Moreover, God knows the ending at the beginning. For God is and was before nothing. What is nothing? Nothing does not exist. God is all-powerful. God is everywhere all the time at the same time. And, God knows everything and all things! Because God created all things in heaven and in the earth by the power of His word! Genesis 1:3 says…And God said let there be light and there was light. And, so, by the power of God's word, light began to exist. God's word is powerful. Hebrews 4:12 says: for the word of God is quick and powerful and sharper than any two-edged sword, piercing even to the dividing asunder of the soul and spirit and of the joints and marrow and is a discerner of the thoughts and intents of the heart. Did you know that God knows our thoughts before they come into our minds? Because it is God who made and created us by His wisdom and power. Psalm 100:3 says: know you that the Lord he is God: it is He that has made us and not we ourselves; we are his people and the sheep of his pasture. Romans 13:1 says: let every soul be subject unto the higher powers: for there is no power but of God; the powers that be are ordained of God! Romans 4:17 says: (As it is written, I have made you a father of many nations) before him whom he believed, even God, who makes the dead alive and calls those things which be not as though they were. Isaiah

44:24 says: Thus said the Lord, your redeemer, and He that formed you from the womb, I am the Lord that makes all things, that stretches for the heavens alone, that spread abroad the earth by myself.

Pain is invisible. We cannot physically see pain, but we can see the effects and symptoms, which cause the pain. And, doctors can diagnose or determine the nature of the illness or sickness. Some, but not all, diseases are detectable. Only God alone knows and understands all symptoms. Not only does He know the symptoms, but He can also heal all manner of sickness and diseases. For nothing is too hard for God because God specializes in dong the things that are impossible. Because with God, all things are possible. Read Matthew 19:26. Moreover, because of God, all things consist and exist.

Hearing is invisible. Hearing is the process or power of taking in sound. It is God who gave us the ability to hear through our ears. It is the inner ear, which consists of the vertebrae organ of hearing. From a sound-transmitting middle ear, that in turn, is separated from a sensory inner. We thank God for our hearing, which is vital to our well-being. Hearing is one of our five sensory abilities.

The wind is invisible. We cannot see the wind, but we can certainly see the power of the wind in a storm or hurricane, in which the wind can be 73 miles per hour and greater, above and beyond that. Did you know that the wind is one of God's treasures? Because God created the wind, God can speak to the wind, and the wind will become calm and still. God can speak to the waves of the raging sea, and the waves of the sea will become calm and still. God speaks to the devil and the demons, and they all obey the voice and the will of God. God is all-powerful for God is the only source of all power. Because God is the beginning and the ending, God knows the ending at the beginning. God is the first and the last. Revelation 1:8 says: I am Alpha and Omega, the beginning and the ending, saith the Lord, which is and which was, and which is to come, the Almighty. God is in complete control of everything and all things because it is and was God who created all things and everything by the power of His word. Whatever God said "let there be" came to be and began to exist because of the power of God's word. Read Genesis, chapters one and two.

The soul and spirit are invisible. Genesis 2:7 says: and the Lord God formed man of the dust of the ground and breathed into his nostrils the breath of life and man became a living soul. And, so the soul of man is the breath of God.

The Holy Spirit is invisible. The Holy Spirit is the working power of God. The Holy Spirit is also the third person in the Godhead. Genesis 1:2 says: and the earth was without form and void and darkness was upon the face of the deep, and the Spirit of God moved upon the face of the waters. John 14:26 says: but the Comforter which is the Holy Spirit, whom the Father will send in my name. He shall teach you all things, and bring all things to your remembrance whatsoever I have said unto you. John 15:26 – But when the comforter is come, whom I will send unto you from the Father, even the Spirit of Truth which proceedeth from the Father. He shall testify of me. Matthew 28:19-20 says: Go you therefore and teach all nations, baptizing them in the name of the Father and of the Son and of the Holy Spirit, teaching them to observe all things, whatsoever I have commanded you, and lo, I am with you always even unto the end of the world. Amen.

Taste is also invisible, but the taste is very essential for nourishment and satisfaction. And, so, some things which are intangible or invisible, are very vital to our well-being and survival or existence. And, let us thank and praise God, the Creator, who created all things visible and invisible. Thank you God for your marvelous works and your everlasting love, mercy, truth, and much, much more. Your blessings, grace, healing, goodness, and protection are inexhaustible, innumerable, and infinite. Praise God from whom all blessings flow!

I Love God Almighty, Jesus, and the Holy Spirit

I love God Almighty because He is the very essence and fiber of my being! It is the truth that I exist because of God. I am alive. I live, move, and have breath in my body because it is God who created me by His omnipotent power. God is the beginning and the ending! God knows the ending at the beginning! God is the first and the last! For from everlasting to everlasting God is God! And, God will always be God! Revelation 1:8 says: I am Alpha and Omega, the beginning and the ending saith the Lord, which is and which was, and which is to come the Almighty. Psalm 90:1-2 says: Lord you have been our living place in all generations before you brought forth the mountains even before you formed the earth and the world, even from everlasting to everlasting, you are God! Genesis 1:1 says: In the beginning God created the heaven and the earth! God is the great I Am! God is self-existent! Everything and all things do exist by and because of the power of God! It is the truth that God is all powerful and God knows everything and all things. Because it is and was God who created and made every thing by the power of His word. Genesis 1:3 says: And God said Let there be light and there was light! And, so, light began to exist or came to be because of the power of God's word. Whatever God said Let there be came to be and began to exist because of the power of God's word! God's word is living and has power! God is everywhere all the time at the same time. God is great and His greatness is truly unsearchable. God is so wonderful, and God and His mercy endures forever to all generations. God is love, and He loves us with an everlasting love! God is the Creator and maker of all things, for God created the things that are visible. God also created the things that are invisible! God is wonderful and most worthy of all praise and thanksgiving. Let everything that has breath praise the Lord. Praise you the Lord!

We must obey and serve God only! We must also worship God in spirit and in truth. John 4:24 says: God is a spirit and they that worship Him must worship Him in spirit and in truth. God Almighty is the one and only true God who created and made the heavens and the earth by the power of His word. God's word is living and has power. God's word will stand forever! Isaiah 40:8 says: the grass will wither, the flower will fade but the word of God will stand forever. Psalm 119:89 says: Forever, O' Lord, your word is settled in heaven. God is synonymous to His word. God is His word. His word is God. John 1:1 says: In the beginning was the word and the word was with God, and the word was God. I love God because He first loved me. And, God will always love me and others. For God loves us with an everlasting love. Jeremiah 31:3 says: The Lord has appeared of old unto me saying, yes, I have loved you with an everlasting love. Therefore, with loving kindness have I drawn you. And, so, we who are born again Christians, have the peace of God. We also have joy, power, love, sound mind, guidance, protection and much, much more. For God so loved the world that He gave His only begotten Son that whosoever believes in Him shall not perish but have everlasting life! Praise God, Jesus, and the Holy Spirit forever and ever. Amen!

Informational Observations

Alcoholism and Drug Addiction

Alcoholism and drug addiction are cancerous and devastating in that these addictions destroy the body inside and out. Long-term use and consumption of drugs, controlled substances, and alcoholic beverages can and will cause strong delusions, false impressions, distortion of the mind in thought and behavior, such as seeing things that are non-existent. People who drink a lot and those who indulge in controlled substances or illegal drugs are in complete denial because they refuse to accept or admit that they have this severe problem of excessive drinking and drug addiction. Their minds and thinking patterns become distorted, erratic, and irrational. They are unable to make rational or sensible decisions. They cannot figure out or decide whether they should go or stay or if they should say yes or no regarding some events or circumstances which occur or happen during their lifetime. Because the causations are so broad and the variables are different.

I have had the experience of living in the same household with both subjects, and it is a sad, pathetic and devastating experience for both parties, the user and the person who is exposed to this type of behavior. On some occasions, they become angry and violent without provocation. And, they are sometimes sad, or cry when there is no apparent reason to do so. They are not self-reliant. They expect and rely on others to do things for them, things which they should and could do for themselves, even simple everyday chores or things common and necessary to maintain or secure good health, etc. They are dysfunctional and not in touch with reality. And, the level of confusion and misunderstanding is unbelievable. The sad part about this kind of situation is that they think those who are trying to help, are wrong. And, they will, with vengeance, accuse those who are trying to help them, of lying about their obvious situation.

They are consistently on the attack and very contrary to necessary correction regarding their bizarre irrational behavior. They are oblivious of the fact that they are the ones who are wrong because of the daily habit of drinking alcohol and drug abuse and/or the using of controlled substances, which distorts and deteriorates the mind and body. And, it will eventually cause death.

Alcohol, drugs, and/or controlled substances change the physical appearance of people. I have personally seen this happen to both male and female, who before they became addicted to alcohol and drugs, they were handsome and beautiful people. But, after they overindulged in alcohol and drugs, they became ugly and distorted and barely recognizable. They cannot concentrate in an orderly manner. They also become deeply depressed and they suffer greatly from severe depression. They are moody, non-responsive, aloof or distant, have no interest or feeling. They are confused and not in touch with reality. Nor are they concerned or cognizant of their surroundings. They are only concerned about one thing, which is getting whatever it takes to achieve the next drink or the things which cause them to become spaced out, high or the lack of having little or no control regarding responsibilities and obligations.

They primarily look for the next drink, fix, or high. And they have no special or specific goals because of their lack of being able to be focused and being able to concentrate on the things, which affect them and others around them, which extend to members of the same household in which they live. They rarely or never even read the newspaper or a book. Their concentration and comprehension is almost non-existent or lies dormant. They move about as if they are in a dazed condition. It is such a pathetic and sad state of affairs. When you talk to them, they refuse to listen, and their attention span is extremely short and spatial. I am not being critical or judgmental. I am merely sharing this information for the purpose of helping others to know the pain and agony and suffering of those who experience the tragedies of these addictions. Perhaps, it may also prevent some one else or others not to become involved in a situation like this because it is a no-win situation. Moreover, it has many other devastating effects and terrible consequences. In some cases, even death can be the end result of being involved in these kinds of activities. Severe tumult, agitation of the mind, and other dire consequences can also be the end result.

Perhaps, at this juncture, we should learn about some of the preventive aspects of this severe disease:

1. Pray and ask God to guide and direct and protect us from exposure to situations such as these and others as well.

2. Proverbs 3:5-6 says: Trust in the Lord with all your heart and lean not unto your own understanding but in all your ways, acknowledge Him, and He will direct your path. For when we pray and ask God with a sincere heart and believe that God will guide and protect us in everything we do, according to the will of God, for God is the beginning and the ending.

God is also the first and the last. God is the source of all power! For God calls those things which be not as though they were. What does this mean? It is defined as: by the power of God Almighty and by His word, which He speaks, things which did not exist, came into existence by the power of God's word. Romans 13:1 says: Let every soul be subject to the higher powers for there is no power but of God, the powers that be are ordained of God! Hebrews 4:12 says: the word of God is quick and powerful and sharper than any two-edged sword penetrating even to the dividing asunder of the soul and the spirit and of the joints and marrow and is a discerner of the thoughts and intents of the heart. Romans 4:17 says…(As it is written, I have made you a father of many nations) before him whom he believed even God who quickens the dead and calls those things which be not as though they were. God is and was before nothing. What is nothing? Nothing does not exist. Genesis 1:1 is living proof that God is and was before nothing. Genesis 1:1 says: in the beginning, God created the heaven and the earth! And, so, based on this first verse written in the Holy Bible, which is God's word, it is evident that God is the beginning and the ending. God is the first and the last. The truth is that God created the heaven and the earth. Genesis 1:3 says: And God said let there be light and there was light. And, so, light came into existence by the power of God's word! Throughout the first chapter of Genesis, whatever God called into being came to be because of the word of God! And, so, God created everything, visible and invisible, by the power of His word! You may ask what are some of the things, which are invisible? The wind is invisible, but we know the wind exists because we can feel the gentle breeze caress our faces on a warm summer day. We can also see the effects of the wind in a storm and in the moving of the leaves on the trees. The mind is invisible. Thought are invisible. We must seek first the kingdom of God and His righteousness, and all these others things will be added unto us. We must trust in the Lord with all our heart and lean not upon our own understanding but in all our ways acknowledge God, and He will direct our path. God will teach us his Holy Word. God's word is holy, and his word is living and has power! But, we must recognize and acknowledge that we need God for our survival because it is God who created us and made us. And, because of God, we move, live, and have our being. The 100th Psalm says: know you that the Lord He is God. It is He that has made us and not we ourselves. We are His people and the sheep of His pasture. Enter into His gates with thanksgiving and into His courts with praise. Be thankful unto Him and bless His name. For the Lord God Almighty is most worthy of praise and thanksgiving. Because truly God is great and greatly to be praised, and His greatness is unsearchable. We must spend more time in praising and thanking God, plus daily reading of the word of God and daily prayer as we are guided by the Holy Spirit. We must meditate in the word of God day and night. Psalm 1:2 says: but his delight is in the law of the Lord and in his law does he meditate day and night. We must put into practice Philippians 4:8: Finally, my brothers, whatsoever things that are true, whatsoever things that are honest, whatsoever things that are just, whatsoever things that are pure, whatsoever things that are lovely, whatsoever things that are of a good report; if there be any virtue and if there be any praise, think on these things. Because we can do all things through Christ which strengthens us. But, my God shall supply all your need according to His riches in glory by Christ Jesus. Now, unto God and our Father be glory forever and ever. Amen.

When we know God and His word, we must also obey God and his word, which is inerrant and infallible. For God's word is settled in heaven. God's word has stability and will never pass away. Isaiah 40:8 says: the grass will wither, the flowers will fade, but the word of God will stand forever! So, when we know God and His word, we must obey God and His word. When we do this, we will live a righteous life, which is pleasing in the sight of God. Because God said: but as he which has called you is holy, so be you holy in all manner of conversation. Because it is written be you holy for I am holy! Those of us, who are Christians, must practice living holy because we have the Holy Spirit to guide and teach us and keep us in the way of holiness. My advice to those of whom I have spoken about in this observation is…you must seek God first, His kingdom, and His righteousness, and all these other things will be added unto you. For God will supply all your needs according to His riches in glory by Christ Jesus.

1. You must hear the word of God as well as read the word of God.

2. You must believe that Jesus Christ is the son of God and that He died for your sins but He rose again on the third day with all power in heaven and in earth given to Him by God Almighty!

3. You must ask God to forgive you for your sins, and you must accept Jesus Christ as your Lord and Savior in that you obey Him and follow His example. He is the only role model, which we all must follow, in order to be right. You must be baptized in the water, keeping in mind that when you sincerely ask

God to forgive you for your sins and you have truly accepted Jesus as you Lord and Savior, God gives to you the gift of the Holy Spirit to teach, guide, and protect you from the devil.

4. You must pray and read the word of God, as you are guided by the Holy Spirit. It is very necessary that you pray every day and night. You must obey God and His word each day, as you are guided and taught by the Holy Spirit of God because when you know God and His word, you will not do those things which are wrong. You must sincerely ask God to help you to understand and obey His word according to His will.

Because God's word is living and has power, God's word is healing and His word comforts and blesses us and gives us right instructions and directions. With God, all things are possible because God can do the impossible. God will never leave us nor forsake us. He will protect us from our enemies because He loves us with an everlasting love. For God so loved the world that He gave His only begotten son that whosoever believes in Him should not perish but will have everlasting life. Praise God from whom all blessings flow.

Our Lost Children

Why are so many of today's children lost? The answer is: As parents and custodians of our children, we have failed to teach and share with our children the holy and righteous word of God on a daily basis, which is nourishment and nutrition for our souls. We must teach our children the importance of knowing God and His word. We must also share with them how very important it is to know and obey God and His word, and to live according to how the word of God tells us and instructs us in the way we must live. We must also put these instructions into practice in our everyday activities and contacts as we interact with others. We must remember to have an attitude of prayer, praise, and thanksgiving unto God. We must be sure at some point and time to share with them the plan of salvation, which is after you have shared with them the word of god as you are guided by the Holy Spirit. You should have them repeat these words: "I believe that Jesus Christ is the only begotten son of Jehovah God, the Creator; God, who sent the Holy Spirit to live in the believers; the Holy Spirit, who is our comforter, guide, and teacher, who will abide with us forever. God, forgive me for my sins. I accept Jesus Christ as my Lord and Savior. Lord, thank you for saving me in Jesus' name. Amen."

We must also continue to do follow up work by encouraging our children to attend church regularly, to become involved in daily bible study at home as well as church, and hang out or be with people who are concerned with and involved in church activities. Most churches have bowling leagues, skating activities, trips, etc. And, these wholesome activities are supervised by Christian adults.

If your children have friends who are not Christians, encourage them to share the word of God with them. And, if they don't want to become involved in church activities with you, don't be influenced to become involved in their worldly activities. If you do become involved, you will sin against God and you will suffer dire or serious consequences because you became involved in sinful activities. And, so, please avoid those kinds of activities! Follow and continue to do what the word of God tells us to do. When you or we read the word of God with the aid of the Holy Spirit, we cannot do wrong for God's Holy Spirit will teach, guide, and help us to understand the word of God. And, the Holy Spirit will keep us and lead us in the path of righteousness. As adults and parents, we must know God and His word so that our children can see the light of Christ Jesus in us as we walk and live by the word of God. We must walk in the power of God's Holy Spirit, and as we walk in the power of God's Holy Spirit, we will not fulfill the lust of the flesh. Galatians 5:16 says: This I say then, walk in the Spirit and you shall not fulfill the lust of the flesh. Romans 8:1 says: There is therefore now no condemnation to them which are in Christ Jesus who walk not after the flesh but after the Spirit! I recommend and encourage you to read the word of God everyday and be sure to pray everyday also.

Our lost children are filled with rage, violence, and they have no respect for parents and other adults. They curse or cuss their parents and other adults standing right in their faces. And, many children or youth hit their parents. They are very disrespectful, mean, and cruel. They seem to enjoy inflicting pain on others. Violence and hurting each other is rampant and most prevalent. They enjoy violent movies, games, etc. The more blood shown in the

WHO IS GOD?

movies, the better they enjoy it. They drink, smoke, do drugs right in front of their parents and other adults. Some have beaten and even killed their parents and others. They are very lazy. They don't have the decency or concern to make their own bed or wash or clean their own room. This is normally done by the parent or parents. Their activities consist of playing games, watching tv, drinking, doing drugs, and hanging out with peers or friends. I say this because I have actually seen these things of which I speak. I find it hard to believe that some parents allow and tolerate this bizarre and unacceptable behavior. And, it can and will be changed with the help and power of God Almighty!

1. We must pray and fast because some things do not change except we fast and pray. Mark 9:17-29, Joel 1:14, Nehemiah 1:4-11

2. We must have complete faith in God as we pray. For without faith, it is impossible to please God. Hebrews 11:6 says: But without faith it is impossible to please God for he that comes to God must believe that He is and that he is a rewarder of them that diligently seek him. Matthew 21:22 says: And all things whatsoever you shall ask in prayer, believing, you shall receive.

3. When we pray, we must know God and His word. We must be faithful in obeying God and His word. We must pray and read the word of God daily as we are guided by the Holy Spirit of God.

4. We must share the word of God with others as we are guided by the Holy Spirit of God. We must know Jesus as our Lord and Savior, and we must follow

His example. Because Jesus is the one and only role model which we all must follow universally, throughout the whole world, including all nations. Matthew 28:18-20 says: And Jesus came and spoke unto them saying, all power is given unto me in heaven and in earth. Go you therefore and teach all nations, baptizing them in the name of the Father and in the name of the Son and in the name of the Holy Spirit, teaching them to observe all things whatsoever I have commanded you. And, lo, I am with you always even unto the end of the world. Amen. For with God, all things are possible. Matthew 19:26 says: But Jesus beheld and said unto them: with men, this is impossible, but with God, all things are possible.

And, so, when we obey God, in doing all the things which He has told us to do, according to His word and will, our children's ways, lifestyle, and behavior will change from disobedience to obedience. But, we must be faithful and diligent. We must pray constantly and read as well as meditate in God's word day and night. We must be steadfast, unmoveable, always doing the work of the Lord for we know that our labor or work for the Lord is not in vain. And, so, let us work while we can, doing good works, for the glory of God. And, let our works be consistent with our behavior, which is having a sincere desire and positive, righteous attitude, doing the will of God as we are guided by the Holy Spirit. And, we will be successful in achieving our goals, which is to please God in all of our ways. And with the power of God, this will be done. Praise God from whom all blessings flow.

Prisons, Penal Institutions and Law Enforcement

This article or observation is written to inspire and invoke a solution to the injustice, inequality, and devastation, as well as the inhumane treatment and conditions which, currently exist and are rampant in our correctional facilities and/or jails. Living conditions for those who are incarcerated are deplorable, to say the least. Some of the inmates sleep on the bare floor! These institutions are rat and roach infested. There are times when the inmates do not have any toilet tissue. I happen to know that this is a fact! Because I have bought cases of toilet tissue and bar soap and taken it to the jail for the inmates. I have also taken food to the jail for the inmates, and the authorities would not permit them to eat the food immediately. They had to wait until those in higher authority told them to eat it! Some of the officers and administrators are cruel, violent, and abusive to the inmates. It is a known fact that some of the inmates have been killed inside of the jail!

The staff is inadequate in the performance of their duties in that they tell you in the notice which you receive from them, to be in court at 9:00am. But, when you are in compliance, as you have been instructed by the notice which you, in fact, received from them, and you arrive at that time, they tell you that the court doesn't convene until 12:30pm. I know for a fact that this is true because I have gone to court on many occasions with people who have had to appear in the court room before the judge. On one occasion, I asked the court clerk why did they tell the person to come at 9:00am when they knew very well that they were not supposed to be in court until 12:30pm? The clerk replied/answered: "Oh, they do that all the time!" I did not consider his answer or statement acceptable or responsible, nor was it amusing and certainly not right! It is wrong and irresponsible to repeatedly give notices to people stating 9:00am when they know very well that they are not due in court until 12:30pm. That is so wrong! And, it's inconsiderate of some of the people who work in these institutions. They are negligent, irresponsible, and do not do their jobs as they should. Nevertheless, the inmates are forced to obey the rules. But, the Sheriff Department does not follow their own rules or instructions. Some of the officers are forced to handle inmates who have AIDS. The authorities don't have the decency to inform or tell the officers that, in fact, the inmates have AIDS. They sometimes learn or find out that some of the inmates have AIDS because some of the inmates tell the officers that, in fact, they have AIDS! Inmates are sometimes checked and searched inside their private body part, including their mouth, rectum, and vagina. At other times, it is necessary for the female officers to take the female inmates to the hospital to have their babies. Sometimes, as soon as the baby is born, the female inmates will escape because the officers are not allowed in the delivery room during delivery. The officers are then blamed because the inmate escaped. They are expected to handle soiled sanitary napkins and on some occasions, when a female officer requests to go home, because she's had a call informing her that her child is sick, the officer in charge refuses to allow her to go home so that she can take care of this medical situation. There are many other situations and issues which are prevalent and need to be addressed and resolved.

We are all accountable and responsible to do our part in helping accomplish and to eliminate these dire conditions and deplorable situations and issues. Thank God that there is a solution for these problems. Yes, even every adverse condition or situation – God is the answer! And, He can and will fix every situation and everything if the people of God will obey God. Pray fervently, faithfully, consistently being on one accord, completely led by the Holy Spirit. We are not alone because God is with us and He will not leave us nor forsake us. God is always with us, and He will fight all of our battles because God is always victorious. And, God cannot fail for with God, all things are possible! Nothing is too hard for God. Because God calls those things which be not as though they were! God said in Jeremiah the 33rd chapter, verse 3: Call unto me and I will answer and show you great and mighty things, which you do not know! God is the beginning and the ending. God knows the ending at the beginning because God is the first and the last. Isaiah 44:6 says: thus said the Lord, the King of Israel, and his redeemer, the Lord of hosts: I am the first and I am the last and beside me, there is no God. Isaiah 44:24 says: thus said the Lord your redeemer, and he that formed you from the womb, I am the Lord that makes all things, that stretches forth the heavens alone, that spread abroad the earth by myself. We must trust in the Lord with all our heart and lean or depend not upon our own understanding but in all of our ways, acknowledge God, and He will direct our paths. We must seek first the kingdom of God and His righteousness and all other things will be added unto us. We must know God in a personal way. We must also obey God and His word. We must read the word of God everyday! And, we must pray everyday as we are guided by the Holy Spirit of God. We must know Jesus Christ as our personal savior and Lord in that we obey Him. And, we must follow His example. Jesus is the only one whom we all must know in a personal way and whose example we must follow. We must pray and fast, and, in our prayers, we must ask God to teach us how to pray as he taught his disciples how to pray. Jesus and his disciples prayed. We are his disciples, and we too, must pray as we are guided by the Holy Spirit of God. We must pray and ask God to guide us and give us instructions concerning how? and what? we must do, as God uses us to help eliminate these devastating conditions and terrible issues, which are rampant. And the authorities completely ignore them as if they don't exist. That is not to say that all of those who work in these institutions are corrupt. Some of the, which are few in numbers, are kind and have compassion and are helpful in assisting the inmates. Those of us, who are Christians, must pray and fast and be available and equipped to do the work of God as we are guided by the Holy Spirit of God.

1. We must put on the whole armor of God, which is the power of God.
2. We must have and use the word of God.
3. We must have the shield of faith.
4. We must share the word of God with others as we are guided by the Holy Spirit.

For we can do all things through Christ who strengthens us, and God will supply all our needs according to His riches in glory by Christ Jesus. Now unto God, our Father, be glory forever and ever. Amen. For the battle is not ours but the Lord's, and He will fight for us. And, through God, we will win the battle and be victorious. The harvest is plenteous, but the laborers are few. We must work while it is day, for when night comes, no one can work. We must be steadfast, unmoveable, always doing the work of the Lord, knowing that our work for the Lord is not in vain. II Chronicles 7:14 says: If my people which are called by my name shall humble themselves and pray and seek my face and turn from their wicked ways, then will I hear from heaven and will forgive their sins and will heal their land. Praise God from whom all blessings flow.

Is It Wrong to Practice Homosexual, Lesbian, and Transvestite Activities?

Yes! And, it is an abomination and is immorally wrong! Leviticus 18:22 says: you shall not lie with mankind as with womankind. It is an abomination. Leviticus 20:13 says: If a man lies with mankind as he lies with a woman, both of them have committed an abomination. They shall surely be put to death. Their blood shall be upon them. Romans 1:26 says: for this cause God gave them up unto vile affections for even the women did change the natural use into that which is against nature. Deuteronomy 22:5 says: The woman shall not wear that which pertains to a man, neither shall a man put on a woman's garment for all that do so are an abomination unto the Lord.

A homosexual is a man who has sex with a man instead of a woman. A lesbian is a woman who has sex with a woman instead of a man. A transvestite is a person who puts on or wears clothes pertaining to or appropriate for the opposite sex; or when a man wears a woman's clothing, or when a woman wears a man's clothing.

It is also wrong to have medical sex changes or have an operation for the purpose of changing your sex from male to female or other changes contrary to God's original design. It is wrong as well as an abomination and it is not the will of God! People are not born with this kind of behavior. It is learned behavior. When a baby is born, he/she learns from the environment where he/she is born. They are influenced by things which happen in their surroundings. I have spoken of cloning in the first chapter of this book.

This, too, is wrong. We cannot duplicate or remake the things which God, the Creator, has already created and made. We, as human beings, do not have the power nor the wisdom. It is the truth that we must rely and depend on God for all of our needs, regardless of what they are. And, so, let us not tamper with or interfere with what God has, in His infinite wisdom and power, created for His glory. God forbid. God set our perimeter or boundary, and we must follow His guideline, rule, or plan for our lives. God is sovereign in that He is all–powerful. He knows everything and all things. He is everywhere all the time at the same time. The truth of the matter is that God is in complete control of everything and all things. Because it is God who created and made everything. God truly is the only source of everything. Romans 13:1 says: Let every soul be subject unto the higher powers: for there is no power but of God: the powers that be are ordained of God. Hebrews 4:12 says: for the word of God is quick and powerful and sharper than any two-edged sword, penetrating even to the dividing asunder of the soul and spirit and of the joints and marrow and is a discerner of the thoughts and intents of the heart. Neither is there any creature that is not made known in His sight, but all things are naked and opened unto the eyes of Him with whom we have to do. Isaiah 44:24 says: thus said the Lord your redeemer and He that formed you from the womb, I am the Lord that makes all things; that stretches forth the heavens alone, that spread abroad the earth by myself. Hebrews 11:3 says: through faith we understand that the worlds were framed by the word of God so that things which are seen were not made of things which do appear. Romans 4:17 says: As it is written I have made you a father of many nations before him whom he believes, even God, who quickens the dead and calls those things which be not as though they were. God is the source of all power. God can speak and a man will lay down and die. God can speak again and that same man will get up and live again. God speaks to the wind and the waves of the sea and the wind and the waves obey God. God speaks to the lightning, and the lightning answers God by saying "Here we are". Everything must obey the voice of God, demons or whatever it be. They all shall obey God's will.

And, so, if we have the sincere desire to be saved and have salvation, we must hear and read the holy word of God. And, we must believe that Jesus Christ is the only begotten son of God and that He died for our sins. We must ask God to forgive us for our sins. And, we must accept Jesus Christ as our personal savior and let Him be the Lord of our lives, in that we obey and serve God only. We must also know Christ Jesus and follow His example, for Jesus Christ is the only role model which we all must follow in order to be right according to the holy word of God, found in the Holy Bible, which is the inerrant, infallible word of God, which is living and has power. We must know God and His word as well as obey God and His holy word. We must pray as we are guided by the Holy Spirit. When we know God and His word and obey God and His word, we will have victory over sin and we will live righteously before God and humanity. Moreover, because we know God and His word and we have the Holy Spirit of God to keep us, teach and guide us, as we walk in the Holy Spirit of God, we will not fulfill the lust of the flesh. Because when we are in Christ Jesus, we are complete. For, in Jesus Christ lived all the fullness of the

Godhead bodily. And, in Him, we are complete, which is the head of all principality and power. Romans 8:1 says: There is therefore now no condemnation to them which are in Christ Jesus, who walk not after the flesh but after the Spirit. And, so, when we know God and His word, we must obey God and His word. We must obey God and His word as we are guided by the Holy Spirit of God. Therefore, we will not do those things, which are an abomination unto the Lord. We know that through Jesus Christ we can do all things because God will supply all of our needs according to His riches in glory by Jesus Christ. Trust in the Lord with all your heart and lean not upon your own understanding. In all your ways, acknowledge God, and He will direct your paths. Seek you first the kingdom of God and His righteousness and all these other things will be added unto you. Pray without ceasing. You shall love the Lord your God with all your heart and with all your soul and with all your strength and with all your mind and your neighbor as yourself – Luke 10:27.

And, in my conclusion, remember to pray and read the word of God everyday as you are guided by the Holy Spirit of God, keeping in mind that you must also obey God and His word at all times. And, share the word of God with others as you are guided by the Holy Spirit of God. You must meditate in God's word day and night so that evil thoughts will not come into your mind. Philippians 4:8 says: whatsoever things that are true, whatsoever things that are honest, whatsoever things that are just, whatsoever things that are pure, whatsoever things that are lovely, whatsoever things that are of a good report; if there be any virtue and if there be any praise, think on these things. We can do it because through Jesus Christ, we can do all things and God will supply all our needs according to His riches in glory by Christ Jesus. Now, unto God and our Father, be glory forever and ever. Amen.

Success

Thanking God Almighty from whom all blessings flow, I greet you in the name of our Lord and savior Jesus Christ and in the name of the Holy Spirit. May the peace of God and His mercy be with you. On February 20, 2003, as I was reading the holy scriptures of God in the book of Isaiah, God gave me the subject for this message, which is success. The scriptural text is found in Joshua chapter 1, verses 1 through 11.

Being a teacher of the word of God, I am concerned and cognizant of the context or meaning of words. Success is to accomplish your goals in life. Number one, it is always necessary to acknowledge God first in all of our ways and He will direct our paths. We must trust in God with all our heart and lean not upon our own understanding. And, we will be successful. Our success is not predicated upon our presence and efforts. But, our success is predicated and based upon the presence and power of God. For the joy of the Lord is our strength. It is most essential and necessary that we know God and His word. And, we must obey God and His word. We must also share the word of God with others as we are guided by the Holy Spirit. We must also serve God only. Joshua chapter one, verses 8 and 9 say: this book of the law shall not depart out of your mouth, but you shall meditate therein day and night, that you may observe to do according to all that is written in the law, for then you shall make your way prosperous and then you shall have good success. Have I not commanded you? Be strong and of good courage. Be not afraid, neither be you dismayed for the Lord your God is with you wherever you go. And, so, the ultimate goal is to seek you first the kingdom of

God and His righteousness and all of these other things will be added unto you. We must trust in the Lord with all our heart and lean not upon our own understanding but in all of our ways acknowledge God, and He will direct our paths. We must press toward the mark for the prize of the high calling of God in Christ Jesus, which is doing the work which God has called us to do for the glory of God as we are guided by the Holy Spirit. And, never give up! Because can do all things through Christ who strengthens us. For my God will supply all of our needs according to His riches in glory by Christ Jesus. To God our Father be glory forever and ever. Amen. For God created us for His glory! And, told us, in His word, to do all things for His glory. I Corinthians 10:31 says: whether therefore you eat or drink or whatever you do, do all to the glory of God.

If we are to be successful, we must ask God for instructions and directions. For the way of success for every endeavor or situation is God. For without God, we cannot do anything or nothing! Because it is God who gives us the ability and strength to breathe His air and to inhale and exhale. When and if we use our mind, which is an entity that is invisible, the mind is our reasoning faculty, which is intangible or invisible. There are other things, which are invisible, the wind, our hearing, our voice, angels are sometimes invisible, our thoughts, and our minds are invisible. And, so, God is the power and the key to our success regardless of the origin or nature of our success. For we must have the wisdom, knowledge, understanding, strength, and power from God, who is the source of all power and everything and all things.

It is the truth that God is the beginning and the ending. Moreover and because God is the first and the last, God is and was before nothing. What is nothing? Nothing does not exist. God is all powerful. God is everywhere all the time at the same time. God knows everything and all things. And, rightly so, because it is and was God who created and made everything! Things that are visible and invisible are created by God. God created everything by the power of His word! Genesis 1:3 says: and God said let there be light and there was light! And, by the power of God's word, light came to be or began to exist because of God's word.

"Be" is the most used verb in the English language because it is an action word. In the beginning, God created the heaven and the earth! Whatever God said let there be – came to be and began to exist because of the power of God's word. And, so, we are totally dependent on God for everything!

God is independent. God does not need us. But, we certainly do need God for our very existence! We cannot live without the help of God. We move, live, and have our being because of God. God is the very source, fiber, essence, reason, and cause. There must be a cause before there is an effect. Listen to this: God is the cause and the effect! Because God is the beginning and the ending. God is the first and the last. For from everlasting to everlasting, God is God. And, God will always be God!

God never slumbers or sleeps. God is infinite. God is eternal. God is love! God is faithful! God is great, and His greatness is unsearchable! God is wonderful! And, He is most worthy of all praise and thanksgiving. And, His name alone is excellent! How marvelous are His works. The heavens declare the glory of God! And, the firmament show His handiwork. Praise you the Lord! Let everything that has breath praise you the Lord!

And, in my conclusion, we depend upon God for everything for it is the truth: We can only be successful when we rely and depend on God for all our needs. God is the reason for our success. Praise God from whom all blessings flow. Amen. May God bless you. Amen.

Time

What is time? It is a biblical truth that God Himself is time! For before there was nothing, God is and was, and God will always be because God is the beginning and the ending. Moreover, He is the first and the last. God is the Alpha and the Omega. God, who is the beginning, stepped out into eternity for God is eternity. And, God is time. Time cannot exist apart from God. God is in complete control of time! Events could not happen or come to pass or be. "Be" is the most important verb in the English language because it is an action word. God used the verb "be" to create the heavens and the earth. In Genesis the first chapter, verse three, we find these words: And God said let there be light and there was light. And, so, because of God's word, light came to be and began to exist based on or because of the power of God's words. Words are very important especially the words of God! For, by the words of God, everything came to be or began to exist based on or because of the power of God's word. Without God and His word, nothing could or would exist or be. Fro the word of God is quick and powerful and sharper than any two-edged sword, piercing even to the dividing asunder of the soul and spirit and of the joints and marrow and is a discerner of the thoughts and the intents of the heart. Just think about that for a moment. God's word divides or separates the soul and spirit and separates the marrow from the bone. And, He knows all of our thoughts even before our thoughts enter our minds. As a matter of truth, God knew we would be in this very room at the beginning before He created the heavens and the earth because God knows everything! And, God is the source of all power! Romans 13:1 says: Let every soul be subject unto the higher powers. For there is no power but of God: the powers that be are ordained of God.

Without time, there would not be any events because there must be a time in order for an event to take place, occur, or happen. Galatians 4:4 says: but when the fullness of time was come, God sent forth His son, made of a woman, made under the law. And, Christ Jesus came at the appointed time and was made flesh. (Galatians 4:4; John 1:1-17)

Time is computed or measured by years, months, weeks, days, moments, sundials, and clocks. Time of events are dated by succession of families (Genesis 5:1-32) and lives of great men (Genesis 6:7, 11), succession of kings (I Kings 11:1-42, 43), earthquakes (Amos 1:1), important events such as the exodus (I Kings 6:1), important emperors (Luke 3:1), periods of time stated in years such as bondage in Egypt (Acts 7:6), the wandering in the wilderness (Deuteronomy 11:2-9; 10:46), the times of the judges (Judges 11:26), the time of captivity (Daniel 9:2, 24, 27), sequence of prophetic events such as the advent of Christ (Mark 1:15; Galatians 4:4), the time of the Gentiles (Luke 21:24), time of the day of salvation (II Corinthians 6:2), the time of the gospel age (Acts 2:17), the time of the last day before the return of Christ (II Timothy 3:1-17; II Peter 3:3-18), the last day of Christ's return (John 6:39, 40-54), the time of the new earth (Revelation 21:1), which is yet to come. Our purpose and goal is to teach and preach the gospel or word of God to as many people as possible, as we are led by the Holy Spirit, for the glory of God.

God is the source of time because God Himself is time! As a matter of truth, God is the beginning and the ending.

God is the first and the last. God is the Alpha and the Omega. God is and was before nothing! What is nothing! Nothing does not exist! And, so, now is the time to be about our heavenly father's business, doing good works for the glory of God while we still have time to do so. We must pray and read the word of God everyday as we are guided by the Holy Spirit of God. We must praise and thank God for His many blessings, healing, salvation, deliverance, protection, provisions, goodness, mercy, grace, peace, joy, wisdom, knowledge, understanding, and much, much more. And, for more time to obey God and to do what we do for the glory of God according to the will of God as we are led by the Holy Spirit of God. Praise God from whom all blessings flow. Thank you, God, for time. Amen.

My Response and Observation to the article written by someone on the subject "Does the Church Have a Future?"

When we speak of the church in regards to the future, the church should have no fear because God is the future, and He holds our future in the palm of His hands. Therefore, we have a wonderful future in Christ Jesus, our Lord and Savior! God said in His holy word: For God has not given us the spirit of fear but of power and of love and of a sound mind (II Timothy 1:7). In regards to change and time, I differ with the author because God is time, and nothing can change except by the power of God, for He transcends time and space. And, without God, there can be no time or change. Moreover, God is the source of everything! Before there was Who? What? Where? When? How? and Why?, God is and God will always be.

"Be" is the most used verb in the English language, and it is defined as "existence or to cause to be or to make", as in Genesis 1:3: And God said let there be light! And there was light! From everlasting to everlasting, God is and always will be! For God is eternal and infinite (Psalms 90:2; Psalms 147:5; Isaiah 40:28). God will change things in His time, for God is the source of all power! Romans 13:1 says: Let every soul be subject unto the Higher powers for there is no power BUT of God. The powers that be are ordained of God!

The writer refers to the "good old days". I believe that every day which God has made, is a good day. It is the things which occur during the day or days that are negative.

Days are classified as: sunny, snowy, rainy, etc., keeping in mind that God is incomplete control of His days (Psalms 74:16). In reference to the many hurting people, God will, in His infinite wisdom, heal our hurts and pains. God said in II Chronicles 7:14: if my people which are called by my name, shall humble themselves, and pray and seek my face and turn from their wicked ways, then will I hear from heaven, and will forgive their sins and will heal their land. When we, as the people of God, humble ourselves and pray and submit ourselves to God, we will overcome (James 4:7; John 16:33). We must not give up because the battle is not ours but the battle is the Lord's (II Chronicles 20:15-26). As the body of Christ, we must reach out in love to help our brothers and sisters who are in need.

According to the will of God, it is essential that we prepare and assure our children of a good, progressive future. The first foundational step is to teach them basic Bible principles and give them scriptural directives and instructions which will help them to cope and deal with the many complex as well as challenging situations which are very prevalent in today's society. We must thank and praise God for having solutions for all of our problems. It is most essential that we share our faith in God with our children. We must demonstrate faith in everyday activities as we interact with them and with others. It is absolutely necessary that they see visible proof of our faith in God by application, based on what we do.

We who are Christians should have no fear in reference to the future because II Timothy 1:7 says: For God has not given us the spirit of fear but of power and of love and of a sound mind. He has also said: I will never leave you nor forsake you (Hebrews 13:5). The Bible also says:

I can do all things through Christ who strengthens me (Philippians 4:13). So, because of Christ Jesus, we have the victory in every situation regardless of the severity of the circumstances. For with God, all things are possible.

And, so, with God, we can look to the future with great expectations, knowing that God is in complete control of our future. For God transcends time and space; and, in Him, we have eternal life, which means we have no need to fear the future because God is the past, God is the present, and God is the future. He will supply our needs according to His riches in glory by Christ Jesus, our Lord and Savior.

My Response and Observation to an Article Written by Someone Regarding African-Americans: "Will Our Past Become Our Future?"

Thanking and praising God from whom all blessings flow, it is right and proper to acknowledge God in all of our ways and He will direct our path. God has commanded us to give thanks in all things (Ephesians 5:20). God is also the object of our praise (Psalm 145; Psalm 148). It is rather unusual to begin a title with an interrogative, but it is interesting. I suppose, with all of the complexities, phenomenon, and unanswered questions which confront us in today's society, some may very well begin articles with interrogatives. Possibly, it was due to the diversity of the bibliographies used by the author of this particular article. I do not agree entirely with the unusual theory expressed by this author in reference to the plight of African-Americans regarding conditions in the past as well as in the future.

The African Americans were and still are a people truly protected, guided, and nurtured by God Almighty, who, in His infinite wisdom and power, never left them, even for a split second; for God said in Hebrews 13:5, Let your conversation be without covetousness and be content with such things as you have for He hath said I will never leave you nor forsake you. I believe that God has taught us to be content regardless of the circumstances because we are to submit ourselves to God, and He will exalt us. Moreover, we must obey and serve God only. We cannot serve two masters. Because we do have God as our Lord and savior, even though we ourselves have nothings, but because of

God, who made the heavens and the earth (Psalms 24; Psalms 136) as well as everything both in the heavens and in the earth (Genesis 1:1, Genesis 2:1), we are rich in Christ Jesus (Philippians 4:19-20). It is true, in past years that we were deprived economically, socially, and educationally, etc. But, because of God's mercy and blessings, we have overcome those weights and hindrances, which beset us in the past. And, because of Christ Jesus, our Redeemer, who died on the cross of Calvary for our sins, and we who have asked God to forgive us for our sins and have accepted Jesus as our Lord and personal savior, we are saved, and in Jesus, we have the victory and power over all things (Philippians 4:13).

God is our emancipator, and He, alone, is responsible for our freedom! In regards to the slave masters, the choices were extremely inhumane: they either obeyed or they were killed. It is crystal clear that they had no rights and were not even remotely considered as human beings.

The author used inserts from the old Negro spiritual hymn "Amazing Grace". Truly it was God's grace and still is the grace of God that will lead us home. In these days, we shop 'til we drop, but during that era, they worked until they dropped. (This information is based on credible historical documentation.) I don't quite agree with the writer's expression or statement that they were a substandard breed of the wrong color. As for the truth of the matter, they were and still are a part of God's wonderful creation in the beginning (Genesis 1 & John 1).

God has prevailed in the past, present, and future of African-Americans. He has sustained and brought us through the fire and through the floods and will continue to teach, heal, protect, and lead us to higher heights of success and completeness in Him, for, in Him, we are complete (Colossians 2:10). Because of Christ, we can and will achieve our goals. The rhetorical question is: Will our past become our future? For in Christ Jesus, we have overcome every stumbling block, and, having spoiled principalities and powers, He made a show of them openly, triumphing over them in it (Colossians 2:15). Moreover, we are successful in every vocation or profession know tot the human race.

In my conclusion, because we are in Christ Jesus and have the Holy Spirit as our guide and teacher, we most assuredly represent the past, present, and the future. God has opened doors for us that were at one point impossible for us to enter. However, with God, all things are possible. Christ Jesus and the Holy Spirit are infinite and eternal. They are the past, present, and future and more, for god is everywhere all the time at the same time; He is all-powerful; God is all knowing. He is Alpha and Omega. God is the source and origin of everything! Let every soul be subject unto the higher powers for there is no power but of God. The powers that be are ordained of God (Romans 13:1). God is our future.

Articles on Marriage…

Neglected Wife

These experiences and impressions that I have set forth on paper are based on my encounters and contacts that I have had with my husband. I am not wanted or respected by my husband; he treats me like dirt! He only has kind words and conversation for his children and relatives. When he is home, he retires to his den and communicates with his tapes, radio, television, and his various machines. Whenever his sexual desires are aroused and no one else is around, he reluctantly turns to me for sexual involvement and to release his pent-up emotions for the moment. No tenderness or endearing words; just a quick release of too much sperm – not caring whether I am satisfied at all or if I receive any gratification.

I long for conversation. Whenever I approach or say something to him, he attacks me angrily and says that I am a bother to him. He remarked that he can only relate to his tapes, his machines, TV, etc. He claims he finds solace and comfort in them.

I am sorry, and I regret that I have caused him so much misery and discomfort. I have tried to be a good wife, but I guess I have not devoted enough time or effort toward the success of the marriage. We seldom do anything together or go places together. It is hard to imagine living in a house with one's own husband and being lonely. He does not try to understand or communicate with me. If I go to him for comfort, or just mere conversation, he remarks: "We have nothing to say to each other."

Someday, God will show us both where we have been wrong. We should be more loving and kind toward each other. Life is too precious to waste with needless heartaches and misery; each day is meaningful and precious and to be lived to the fullest. We should show the utmost kindness to each other. Married couples should never go to bed or asleep angry with each other. They should discuss the matter and resolve it! Apologize to each other for whatever misery or wrong that was caused by the other or any misery that caused the other party to experience suffering and needless pain.

If God is put first in the lives of every couple or family, things will be resolved in a way that is meaningful and advantageous to everyone involved; but only if God is included in all phases of our lives!

I have fond memories of the long-ago times when we were honest with each other. We were able to talk about anything to each other; we talked about our dreams and planned our future together. At this stage or point in the marriage, we are unable to relate to one another. There is little or no communication because of the animosity that exists coupled with competitive attitudes. It is just impossible to carry on a constructive and meaningful conversation; it inhibits my spontaneity! I am afraid of being yelled at or criticized or being told that I am lying or covering up. I long for pleasant conversation and just to be able to pour out my heart and talk about things that have developed over a long period concerning family matters. But, I must content myself with the fact that the only thing left to do, at this point, is to suppress my feelings as well as my impressions. I would like to go to my husband and pour out my heart, but he makes this almost impossible. He does not share things concerning his life with me. He prefers to share them with others of his choosing – things that should, in fact, be shared only with me. I feel very inhibited almost to the point of being afraid to speak out concerning issues that distress me. He complains and accuses me of keeping things or not discussing things with him, but he does not discuss things of importance with me. He also keeps or withholds many things within the home from me.

I sincerely believe the only way a couple can have a successful and meaningful marriage is:
- To be completely honest with each other; and
- To trust each other and share everything with each other.

My husband does not respond to negative criticism in a positive and realistic way. He has a tendency to cover up and avoid most of the negative incidents. In this life, one must view and analyze the negatives as well as the positives. For, if we never experience any negative things, how can we appreciate the positive things?

(more later..)

Observations During a Traumatic Experience

My inability to speak is due to a psychological impasse or psychosomatic syndrome. It was brought on or caused by a phone call from my husband. During this phone call, he engaged in many merciless, vicious, and false accusations and verbal abuse and character assaults in regards to me. The impact of this cruel attack has caused the ego to recede or digress. Therefore, if the ego is inoperable, the id refuses to function because the id depends on the impulses of the ego. The ego is supposedly the most important component of the psyche.

I am fine, and I am also fully aware of my surroundings or environment. There is no need for surveillance, as I shall not become violent. The recent occurrence was a very traumatic experience. The psyche, at present, is functioning silently. If properly nurtured, it will again be restored to a state of normality. Please!! Do not get upset or exhibit or show fear. This will only intensify the matter or situation. Please exercise some patience. Things are going to work out fine. If you so desire, you may ask questions, and I will answer them in written form. Thank you, and may God bless you all.

Trust

(The latter part or section of this paper is of a rather personal nature, based on my true feelings and observations.) You can never trust me or any other woman, or anyone, for that matter, simply because of your deep-seated unbelief. And, if you don't change your concepts in reference to life and reality, you will always be a most miserable person. Your concepts of wanting to mold your woman or people, for that matter, to suit your specifications or needs – this is an unnatural desire. Accept people on the basis of their very own merits. Our marriage will never mean very much to you if you continue to place your pride and scholastic achievements and other priorities above the marriage. Continuing to dig for things merely for the purpose of humiliation and to try and confirm your unfounded suspicions (manufactured by your own mind). But, to you, these suspicions are real. Things that you so boldly accused me of are incredible! For example, the Alderman situation – accusing me of trying to put myself on him. You also said that I tried to go to bed with him, none of which is true and none of this is true!

I have never forced my affections upon anyone for I am too much of a lady to stoop that low! You also accused me of having affairs with many other men and being yet obligated to this day for things which these men have done for me. I don't see how you can make a statement like that, when, in fact, you have been the recipient of my unselfish love. I have sincerely tried to be the kind of wife you have needed but with little success because you refuse to believe that there are women in this world that do not commit adultery, that are not sneaks and are not out for monetary gain.

The things that I have achieved were ascertained by the sweat of my brow – many years of hard work to the point of working two jobs, saving whenever I could so that I could have something to call my own without being obligated to some one else.

(more later..)

Marriage Conflicts

Some of my observations and feelings set forth here on paper at this time are geared solely for the purpose of trying to express my true feelings regarding my recent marriage. Upon marrying Mr. McIntyre, the man who is now my husband, the marriage started with a feeling of ecstasy, a feeling of delight, trust and serenity. The quiet moments we shared together, oblivious of our surroundings, locked in each other's arms, lost in deep meditation, reminiscing, loving, feeling the undying need of our love for each other; being honest with each other; it has been a cleansing process. Refreshing, rewarding, but I must be honest and try, in the best way I know how, to deal with reality. To admit one's own faults and shortcomings takes strength and faith in God. I have complete faith in God. If it were not for my undying faith in God, my sanity would have crumbled long ago. Because I have had many tears and sorrows because of how some people have deceived me.

Most people find it almost impossible to believe that I can make this statement saying that "I truly love everyone regardless of race or origin, or whether or not this love is returned – it does not matter." "If love is not returned to me by the recipient of my love, I am still going to love people because this is one of God's commandments." "Love ye on another as I have loved you." To have a friend, it is essential that you be a friend. It is also essential that you look for the good in people and expound the manifestation of that goodness. (more about that later...)

Getting back to our marriage, the marriage started off with a deep abiding love, total concern for the other's overall welfare; being able to tell each other everything;

communicating totally with each other; revealing our most inner feelings; a deep-seated emotional unveiling; feeling that no one else had been able to stimulate or inspire. It has been a kind of cleansing experience for both of us to be able to reveal the unspoken sentiments and feelings that had been lying dormant for years just waiting to be discovered. These early days were happy and complete, memories to be treasured and shared by the two people involved. If I were to ever write a book, it would be about love: first, the love that God has for mankind – so great a love that he gave his only Son to die for each of us so that we could have joy and eternal life. Love is everything because "God is love."

I love my husband, but sometimes he makes it difficult to express because of his arrogant, superior attitude. I suppose this air of superiority might be attributed to his sometimes inability to communicate with me and perhaps others also. This can be very frustrating to anyone. One of the major problems in our marriage is Mac's inability to trust me. I have had many moments of sadness because of this. It is very difficult to cope with and live with especially when the accusations are unfounded and there are no bases for such actions – they are all imagined and imaginary and manufactured by the believer. Take the example of the experience with the Alderman – a very innocent situation geared solely toward helping my brother obtain a job. My husband took the incident out of its original context and added his own concept, which was wrong and incorrect. He accused me falsely of having an affair with the Alderman, and having absolutely no facts regarding the situation, he immediately called the Alderman in a mad rage to establish the validity of his unfounded, uncalled-for accusations.

Take another incident of his mistrust and jealousy: He has made calls and contacted many of my friends and associates regarding their relationship with me in order to try and establish his unreal accusations and feelings about me. In spite of all the calls and contacts, he has been unable to substantiate his outlandish, unreal accusations based on his sinister thoughts and the manifestations of these evil thoughts. If he does not begin to gear his thought pattern toward useful and beneficial things – things of value, constructive things, and good thoughts instead of negative, degrading things designed to destroy and hurt others – I say this because I am the recipient of such hurt – my children are affected by this because they want us to be happy. My children have always loved and respected me as their mother and will do anything that is right to achieve this ultimate goal. I have a deep and profound love for all of my children and will go to the limit for each of them, including my sons-in-law. I try not to show partiality regarding my children. I love Mac's children and would not mistreat them in any way – although, I have been accused of doing this reprehensible thing by my husband. This cuts and hurts deeply to have to live with the fact that your own husband thinks such horrible things about you – especially, when it is not true! Sometimes, I lay awake at night, finding it difficult to sleep because of these accusations and thoughts directed and forced upon me by my husband; the pressures of these things are beginning to take its toll and is noticeable in my appearance and behavior. It is also affecting my health. I am weary of trying, but I must keep going and trust in God to help me through my many crises! Sometimes, my heart is heavily-burdened so much that I feel like giving up, but God gives me the necessary strength to keep pressing onward.

My husband even dug into my previous medical history in order to find things to hurt me and make feel inadequate. He claims he wants to know everything about me solely because he loves me and wants to share everything with me. But, this is not true. He only wants to try and confirm his false accusations. He thinks I have deep, dark secrets, which he can unfold and open the doors of my mind and cleanse my very soul. What he doesn't realize is that he is trying to do the impossible for mankind.

I am very glad that only God can probe and penetrate the soul because He made the soul and constructed it so, He, alone, can understand its functions. In my distress, I call on the Lord, and He always comes to my rescue and relieves me of all my problems no matter how big or small. I am so glad that I know Him and trust Him with all of my problems. I pray that He will continue to be with my family and me, my friends and all of those who desire His presence.

Meanwhile, back to the marriage problem. My husband's sensitivity toward his visual handicap can be very upsetting to others, especially when they mean well and sincerely want to help. Their efforts are perceived with scrutiny and doubt. I realize that being blind is a very difficult thing to live with and to accept – a world of darkness and feelings. People don't understand this in depth, but I personally understand a great deal more than my husband gives me credit for. I would never do anything that would hurt him in any way. If I did, I could never live it down because I sincerely want to help my husband in any way that I can. But, he does not believe this! I go out of my way to do special things to please him, for example, buying special food for him, picking up a pair of pants, sweaters, shirts, etc. and other items I think he might like – things he had previously indicated or expressed a desire to have or need. This may sound negative, but he sometimes goes so far as to take the mail and notes, messages he thinks I have written or received, in order to find out whether or not I have been engaging in any activities unbecoming of a wife, mother, and Christian, so that he can expound and elaborate, criticize, evaluate, cleanse, revitalize, and rejuvenate my very soul. He says he loves me, but how can he love me when he doesn't believe in me, doesn't trust me, has no respect for my rights as a person or wife? This kind of action is displayed quite often. For example, when I relate an incident to him regarding the children, he does not believe me. He has to have a confirmation from his children. He would be utterly shocked at some of the things I could relate to him regarding his children. Many times, I have swallowed and suppressed, yes, yes, even buried within my subconscious mind simply because I know he will not believe me. I suffer physical and emotional scars from these suppressions. There was a time when I could relate to him, but now I find it almost impossible to communicate and relate because he closes his mind and becomes insensitive and oblivious of my needs and desires. I think it is because he has been under a lot of mental and emotional stress and strain, stemming from his job. Extra duties and responsibilities have been literally thrown at him in order to secure his position as one of the administrator for the Central YMCA College. He is forced to accept these added responsibilities, which I feel (in my opinion) are too much coupled with the fact that he has all of these imaginary problems manufactured by and in his own mind – but, in his mind and judgment, it is a reality! I wish there was some way that I could help him because I love him and need him; but he has shut me out of his plans and life because he says that I "don't understand". I understand that he is a very prideful individual when it comes to his principles and his standards that he has set forth for himself. He will die defending them, even though they sometimes offend and hurt others. He believes that his children can do no wrong regardless of what anyone else says – he makes this known to his children, which makes them take a superior negative attitude. It makes them lie needlessly. As long as he continues to treat them in the present fashion, they will never grow up and be able to cope with the world and people because they rely and depend on him too much. They have an affection for him that is somewhat unnatural and dangerous. These feelings between them are very mutual, but he will not face up to these truths. He says that these are all blatant lies, imagined and dreamed up by me. But, people who are not members of our family have also made the same observations.

He says that I am confused and lie a lot. However, this is also true of him. An illustration of this was the time we discussed the visitation of the children. His former wife "sometimes uses me as a babysitter" for their children whenever it suits her purpose. On this particular day, we (Mac and I) discussed the children's visitation rights. We agreed that we would have the children over only on Sundays from twelve pm to six pm. This agreement has been violated several times. One morning, he called me at home, from office, and said that he wanted to have the children over for two weeks during the summer. I agreed.

Upon their arrival, I immediately began to pick up after them – clothing, wash cloths, towels, food, dishes, etc., constantly cleaning the rug and the floor because they come into the house with muddy feet. When they eat, they refuse to clean up after themselves. I am constantly cleaning up after them. When I speak to them, he says I am picking on them. In reality, I am only trying to teach them the things that they should already know as girls who are almost eleven years old. Many things that they should and could do, their father does *for* them. I love his children and will do anything for them, but I am tired and exhausted from working two jobs – maintaining a household of eight, attending community and civic meetings, conventions, etc., visiting hospitals, nursing homes, private homes, court rooms, etc. I cannot afford to raise any more children because of my health. My children will not allow me to keep my grandchildren because they are concerned about the care of my health, because they say after thirty years of babysitting, (incidentally, I started babysitting as a young child for my brothers, sisters, and the neighbors' children) since they think in view of my past years as a babysitter, I need a rest. And, those are also my sentiments. That is why God is blessing me in getting along so well without working because I have spent many years of hard work, trying to support my family in addition to helping others. Now, I truly believe that God wants me to do some missionary work for Him. With His help, I am going to try and achieve the goals that God has planned for me – whether it be preaching, teaching, singing, witnessing, visiting the sick, jails, whatever work He has for me. With His help, I am going to try and be faithful to my calling.

Lately, I have been depressed to the point that it is visible even in my physical appearance. The children have started to ask questions in reference to my health. If I could just get Mac to face the fact that I am not always right; neither is he, nor anyone for that matter. But, I strive to do that which is right and fair. I don't want to take away any love that Mac has for his children. I just want the proper recognition and respect as a wife. The way things are now, I am last, if a decision is made between me and his kids. He would choose the kids because he has said as much – more than once. I shall always remember the day he literally asked me out of his house. He would never say that to his kids, yet, he said it to his wife. I don't feel that I have very much to say regarding the discipline of the children. He makes it very clear that these are his children and "hands-off!" But, I want him to discipline my children, and he sometimes does when he deems it necessary.

Unless things change, the marriage is going to get progressively worse. Already, I am becoming more withdrawn, although, normally, I am, by nature, very warm and outgoing. These are not only sentiments in reference to me, but have been expressed by others as well.

In reasoning with children, you don't have to be harsh. You can show children the love you have for them without smothering them with love. When there is an occasion in time, you should punish them – you should not smooth over the problem by telling them or allowing them to think that what they did was right and that you approve. Because they turn on the tears, you must be firm no matter how it hurts and let them know when they are wrong! If this is not practiced, they will never deal fairly with others later on in life. They will expect the same treatment out in the world, but the world will not be as receptive in its treatment of them. And, the realization of this will be shocking and painful. (more about that later..)

Sermons

What Is a Sermon?

A sermon is a message from God. Moreover, the contents of a sermon must come from God Almighty, who is the Creator, who made and created the heavens and the earth. God created everything! Things that are visible and things that are invisible. God is the beginning and the ending. God is the first and the last. God is the source of all power! For before there was Who? What? Where? When? How? or Why?, God is! As a matter of truth, God existed before nothing. For God was and did exist before nothing. What is nothing? Nothing does not exist or is not. Romans 13:1 says: Let every soul be subject unto the higher powers. For there is no power but of God: the powers that be are ordained of God. God is the great I Am. I Am is a title or name, which refers to God Almighty. (Genesis 17:1, Revelation 19:15) For God is all-powerful, and God knows everything! And, God is everywhere all the time at the same time. God is infinite, eternal, and forever! God transcends time and space for God Himself is time and space. For without God, there would not be time or space because God is from everlasting to everlasting. God is all mighty. God walks upon the wings of the wind and God makes even the clouds his chariot. (Psalm 104:3) God speaks to the lightnings, and the lightnings answer God by saying: Here we are. (Job 38:35) God speaks to the raging sea, and the sea becomes calm and still. God speaks to the wind, and the wind obeys God. Everything obeys God! Demons obey God! What a mighty God we serve! The Lord our God is omnipotent. The Lord our God – He is wonderful. How wondrous are His works! God is great, and His greatness is unsearchable.

And, so, number one, the contents of a sermon must come from the Holy Word of God Almighty, which is found in the Holy Bible! The Bible was written by holy men who were chosen by God to pen or write His holy word as they were guided by God's Holy Spirit. II Peter chapter one, verses 20-21 says: Knowing this first that no prophecy of the scripture is of any private interpretation. For the prophecy came not in old time by the will of man: but holy men of God spoke as they were moved by the Holy Spirit.

Secondly, we must rely on God's Holy Spirit to guide us and to help us to understand the word of God. Because human intellect can not comprehend or understand the word of God!

Step number three: we must first pray and ask God to give us wisdom and knowledge so that we will be able to understand and rightly divide the word of truth which is God's Holy Word! For the word of God is eternal and forever! For without the wisdom of God, we cannot learn or obtain knowledge because the wisdom of God gives us the ability to learn and understand the things we read and do. And, so, without God, we are helpless and without power or energy. But, thanks be unto God, who gives to us power and energy to do things for the glory of God. For God has created us for His glory. We must do all things (which we do) for the glory of God! Isaiah 43:7 says: even everyone that is called by my name for I have created him for my glory. I have formed him. Yes. I have made him! I Corinthians 10:31 says: Whether therefore you eat or drink or whatever you do, do all for the glory of God!

Step number four: We must be called or chosen by God to preach and teach the Holy word of God. John 15:16

says: You have not chosen me, but I have chosen you and ordained you, that you should go and bring forth fruit and that your fruit should remain: that whatsoever you ask of the Father in my name, He may give it to you.

Step number five: It is also necessary that we become yielded vessels for God, and we must surrender our heart, soul, mind, and body unto the guidance and teaching of the Holy Spirit of God, as we study and preach the Holy word of God!

Number six: We must know God and His word in order to teach and preach the word of God. If we do not know God and His word, how can we teach and preach His word? We must pray and study the word of God everyday, so that we will be equipped and prepared to share the word of God with others, as we are guided by the Holy Spirit of God!

Number seven: We must also obey the word of God ourselves so that others can see Christ in us for Christ is the one and only example whom we all must follow in order to be righteous or right. Because Jesus Christ is the way, the truth, and the life. No man comes unto the Father but by Him. John 14:6 says: Jesus said unto him: I am the way, the truth, and the life. No man comes unto the Father but by me.

And, so, in my conclusion, when we label our subject or call it a sermon, it must contain the Holy word of God in order to be named or called a sermon. Those of you who are preachers or messengers of God's word, must use the contents from the bible, which is the inerrant, infallible word of God! If you do not use the word of God for a sermon, please do not call it a sermon! Label or call it a discourse, lecture, or speech. Christ, the Master teacher, used the word of God when He taught or preached. Matthew 4:4

says: But He answered and said: It is written, man shall not live by bread alone, but by every word that proceeds out of the mouth of God. Also, you should read the fifth and sixth chapters of Matthew.

And, so, when you preach a sermon, please use the word of God from the Holy bible, which is the word of God. II Timothy 3:16 says: All scripture is given by inspiration of God and is profitable for doctrine, for reproof, for correction, for instruction in righteousness. May God bless you eternally. Praise God from whom all blessings flow. Amen.

In The Beginning, God Created the Heaven and the Earth

The subject for this sermon is found in Genesis, the first chapter, verse one, which is: In the beginning, God created the heaven and the earth. Thanking God from whom all blessings flow. The subject of this sermon is most unusual because it began with God Almighty, God, who is the only true and living God! For God is the first and the last. He is the beginning and the ending, the Alpha and Omega. Moreover, God is the source and the power by which all things consist and exist. Romans 4:17 says: As it is written, I have made you a father of many nations, before Him whom he believed, even God, who quickens the dead and calls those things which be not as thought they were. What does this mean? Well, before there was nothing, God created everything by the power of His word. For God is the beginning and the source of all power.

In Genesis chapter one, verse three: And God said let there be light, and there was light. And, so, the truth of the matter is the light came to be or began to exist by the power of God's word. Hebrews 4:12 says: For the word of God is quick and powerful and sharper than any two-edged sword, piercing even to the dividing asunder of the soul and the spirit and the joints an marrow, and is a discerner of the thoughts and intents of the heart. Romans 13:1 says: Let every soul be subject unto the higher powers; for there is no power but of God: the powers that be are ordained of God!!!

And, so, God is omnipotent, being all-powerful. God is omnipresent, being everywhere all the time at the same time. For God transcends time and space. God Himself is time. Without God, there would be no time. God is omniscient, in that God knows everything! And, rightly so, and true, because it is and was God who created and made everything. We shall take a solemn look at Genesis 1:1.

Genesis 1:1 is the most profound scripture in the Bible because it is the first verse contained in the Bible. Moreover, it introduces God, who is the Creator! In the beginning, God created the heaven and the earth, by the power and grace of God, let us take a closer look at these first ten words in the holy word of God. "In" is a functional word indicating a manner, state of being, purpose, situation, influence, and power. "In" represents God because God is the "In"! God is also the "the". "The" is the only definite article of the three main articles. "A" and "An" are the two indefinite articles. God is the one and only true and living God!!! "Beginning" – God is the beginning, the First and the Last; the Alpha and the Omega! Before God Almighty, there was no god formed; neither shall there be after, for from everlasting to everlasting, God is God! Before there was Who? What? Where? When? How? and Why? – God is!

God is the who, the what, the where, the when, the how, and the why. God has always been God, and God will always be God! "Be" is the most used verb in the English language because it means that we have life; we live, move, and exist by the power of God Almighty! As you know, "be" is an action word. For in the beginning, God said let there be light, and there was light. Light came to be or began to exist by the power of God's word. God is the beginning. "It" is a biblical historical truth, that God created the heaven and the earth. God is and was before nothing, and because of God who created and made all things, all things came to be because of God's power. Before you can have an effect, there must be a cause. Well, God is the cause and the effect because God is and was before everything. And, it was God who created everything by His power. God stretched out the north over the empty place and hang the earth upon nothing. "Created" is the power of God. "Heaven" is the place where God lives or His dwelling place. "The" earth is God's footstool. God is in complete control of everything, both visible and invisible. God is the Who? What? When? How? and Why? "It" is the truth that God is the beginning and the ending, the First and the Last, the Alpha and the Omega. God is infinite. God is eternal and forevermore. God never slumbers nor sleeps. God is from everlasting to everlasting. He is the lily of the valley, the bright and morning star; and by Him, all things consist and exist. God is love. God is light. God is power. And, we move and live and have our being in God. God is our all in all. We inhale and exhale because of God's power. We are blessed and healed because of God's everlasting love wherewith He loves us. We have a wonderful Lord and Savior, who is Jesus Christ, the righteous. We are the children of God, and we have eternal life through Jesus Christ, our Lord and Savior. Because of God, we are able to awake every morning. Because of God, we have the Holy Spirit, who is our Teacher, our Guide, and our Comforter, who will abide with us forever. Thank you, Jehovah Lord God Almighty for all of your blessings, which are many. Thank you for your gifts; for everything that we have received are gifts. We are blessed because of your goodness, mercy, and love. Thank you for your amazing grace, which is sufficient for every situation.

Thank you for your eternal protection and mercies that are new every morning and your compassion, which fails not. Your mercy endures forever to all generations. Thank you for being our God, who is the Father of our Lord and Savior, Jesus Christ. Thank you for the Holy Spirit, our Comforter. Lord God Almighty, we love you. We adore you. We praise you. We thank you. In the beginning, God created the heaven and the earth. For God is the beginning, the first and the last, the Alpha and the Omega. For from everlasting to everlasting, God is God. Praise God from whom all blessings flow.

Eternal Life!

This message was given to me by God Almighty. The subject of this sermon is eternal life! The scriptural text is found in the gospel of John, the 17th chapter, verses 1-26. Perhaps, at this juncture, we should define or explain the meaning of eternal life. Eternal means everlasting, without end. Eternal is also from everlasting to everlasting. For God and Christ and the Holy Spirit of God – they are eternal. Because God is the beginning and the ending. God is the first and the last. God is the Alpha and the Omega. Jesus Christ and the Holy Spirit were with God before creation and during creation. (Genesis 1:1-3-26) And, God said: Let there be light and there was light. And, so, based on the power of God's word, light came to be or began to exist. "Be" is the most used verb in the English language because "be" is an action word. Whatever God said "let there be.." came to be or began to exist because of the word of God Almighty! "Be" is a derivative of I Am. God referred to Himself as I Am. When God told Moses to go to Egypt and tell Pharaoh to let my people go, Moses asked God: "Who shall I say has sent me?" And, God said unto Moses: I Am that I Am. And, he said: "You shall say unto the children of Israel – I Am has sent me unto you." This title belongs to God, and it means "self-existing". God is the Great I Am. I Am was before "be" because it is and was God who said: Let there be. And, because of I Am, who is God, "be" came to be. Without I Am or "be", you can't have the other helping or auxiliary verbs, which are have, had, was, been, are, and is. First of all, you have to be because be means life; if you don't "be", then you don't exist. We move, live, and have our being because of God.

Moreover, without God, we cannot do anything. Without God, we are helpless. Without God, we cannot breathe or awake or go to sleep. It is God who causes us to go to sleep and awake each morning. Scientists have been doing sleep studies for years, trying to find out the process for going to sleep. They still have not discovered that process. Only God knows the procedure. And, only God is able to perform that procedure. Some people believe that alarm clocks wake them up, but if God does not wake us up, we will sleep into eternity. But, thanks be to God that He does wake us each day.

At this point or juncture, by the power and grace of God, I shall elaborate on the subject eternal life. We only have eternal life through our Lord and Savior Jesus Christ, who is the only begotten son of God.

1. We must hear or read the word of God.
2. We must believe the word of God.
3. We must confess or admit that we have sinned.
4. Ask God to forgive us for our sins. And, verbally accept Jesus Christ as our personal Lord and Savior.

Jesus is the only way of eternal life. Jesus said in John 14:6: I am the way, the truth and the life. No man comes to the Father but by me. Acts 4:12 says: neither is there salvation in any other for there is no other name under heaven given among men whereby we must be saved. And, so, in order to have salvation and eternal life, you must, as an individual, confess or say these words: *Dear God, forgive me for my sins. I believe that Jesus Christ is the only begotten son of God and that He died for my sins. But, He rose again on the third day, with all power in heaven and in earth in His hands, given to Him by God. I accept Jesus Christ as my Lord and Savior. Please, be the Lord of my life and help me to obey and serve God, Christ, and the Holy Spirit of God. Teach me the word of God. Give me wisdom, knowledge, and understanding of your word. Help me to remember to pray and read your holy word each day as I am guided by your Holy Spirit. Order my steps in your word. Open my eyes that I may behold wondrous things out of your law. Help me to walk in the path of righteousness for your great name's sake. In Jesus' precious name, I pray. Amen.*

Eternal life is the gift of God through His son Jesus Christ. For God so loved the world that he gave His only begotten son that whosoever believes in Him should not perish but have everlasting life. We cannot work for salvation or eternal life. Ephesians 2:8-9 says: For by grace are you saved, through faith and that not of yourselves. It is the gift of God, not of works lest any man should boast. But, in order for us to have eternal life, God gave His only begotten son to die on the cross of Calvary for our sins. Jesus was sinless and without sin. He gave His perfect life for the sins of the whole world. He died an agonizing, painful death. He was lied on, beaten, and they even spit on Him. But, Jesus Christ suffered all of this for all of us, so that we can have eternal life through Jesus Christ, our Lord and Savior. No one took Jesus' life. He willingly gave His life for us. And, those of us who have asked God to forgive us for our sins and who believe that Jesus Christ is the only begotten son of God and that He died for our sins, and we have accepted Jesus Christ as our Lord and Savior, are saved. And, we have eternal life through our Lord and Savior, Jesus Christ. As Christians, we must seek ye first the kingdom of God and His righteousness, and all other things will be added unto us. We must trust in the Lord with all our heart and lean not upon our own understanding but in all our ways, acknowledge God, and He will direct our path. We must keep our mind stayed on the Lord, and He will keep us in perfect peace. We must obey and serve God only. We must walk in the Holy Spirit of God, and we will not fulfill the lust of the flesh. Romans 8:1-2 says: There is therefore now no condemnation to them which are in Christ Jesus, who walk not after the flesh but after the Spirit. For the law of the Spirit of life in Christ Jesus has made me free from the law of sin and death. God has given us the instructions for living a righteous life. Philippians 4:8 says: Finally my brethren, whatsoever things are true, whatsoever things are honest, whatsoever things are just, whatsoever things are pure, whatsoever things are lovely, whatsoever things are of a good report, if there be any virtue, if there be any praise, think on these things. If you still have a problem, move on to the 13th verse, which says: I can do all things through Christ who strengthens me. And, if you still have a problem, move to verse 19-20: but my God shall supply all your needs according to His riches in glory by Christ Jesus. Now unto God, our Father, be glory forever and ever. Amen. We have this blessed assurance that Christ is even at the right hand of God making intercession for us.

    And, in my conclusion, who shall separate us from the love of Christ? Shall tribulations or distress? Or persecution? Or famine? Or nakedness? Or peril? Or sword? As it is written, for thy sake, we are killed all the day long. We are counted as sheep for the slaughter. No, in all these things, we are more than conquerors through

Him that loved us. For I am persuaded that neither death, nor life, nor angels, nor principalities, nor powers, nor things present, nor things to come, nor height, nor depth, nor any other creature, shall be able to separate us from the love of God, which is in Christ Jesus, our Lord. Walk on by faith in God. Praise God from whom all blessings flow. We have eternal life through Jesus Christ, our Lord and Savior. May God bless each of you eternally.

Authority, Eternity, and Infinite

Thanking God from whom all blessings flow, I greet you all in the name of God, Christ, and the Holy Spirit. And, may God's blessings be upon each of you. The subject of this sermon is: Authority, Eternity, and Infinite. The scriptural text is from the book of Isaiah chapter fifty-seven, verse fifteen, Psalms 90:1-2, Isaiah 43:10-13, Isaiah 4:6-6, and other supporting scriptures. What is the definition of authority? Authority is lawful or legal right to enforce obedience. What is eternity? Eternity is time without end or infinite time – the state of being eternal, endless. How shall we define infinite? Infinite is being without limits of any kind or limitless. God is all three. He is the absolute first and final authority. Before God brought forth atom and matter, God is! Before God created the heavens and the earth, for the earth abides forever. (Psalm 104:5) God is! God was! And, God will always be! And, God will always exist and live! God is eternal and forever! For from everlasting to everlasting, God is God! God is infinite! What is an atom? An atom is energy or power. An atom is composed of the smallest particle of an element that has the properties of the element and can exist either alone or in combinations. What is matter? Matter is the physical substance of the universe, something that occupies space and has weight. God is all of the above because God is the source of everything! God is the beginning and the ending. God is the first and the last. God is the Alpha and the Omega. Before there was When? Where? What? Who? How? and Why?, there is and was God. God is the Who? What? Where? When? How? and Why? God stepped out into eternity, endless time, time that never ends, for God, Himself, is time. God is eternity! God is the ultimate first and final authority! God is infinite. God is eternal, for from everlasting to everlasting, God is God! God lives in eternity because God is eternity! The authority and the powers that be are of God. Romans 13:1 says: Let every soul be subject unto the higher powers for there is no power but of God. The powers that be are ordained of God! But, wait a minute. Let us consider the trinity, which is God Almighty, who is the Father; Jesus Christ, who is the son of Jehovah God, to whom God has given all power in heaven and in the earth, who is the savior of the whole world, the everlasting Father, the Prince of peace, the Messiah, the King of kings, and the Lord of lords. He is the Light of the world, the Bread of life, the Water of life, the Master Teacher, the Greatest Physician or Doctor, the Healer of all kinds of sickness and diseases. Jesus is the second person in the Godhead. (Colossians 2:8-10) the third person in the Godhead or trinity is the Holy Spirit, the Comforter, who is our teacher and our guide. The Holy Spirit is the working power of God, whom God sent into the world to live in the believers, Christians, or followers of Jesus Christ.

1. You must hear the word of God.
2. You must believer the word of God.
3. You must repent and ask God to forgive you for your sins.
4. You must accept Jesus Christ as your Lord and Savior in that you obey Him and follow His example.

Jesus is the one and only role model, which we all must follow in order to be right and live a righteous life. You must be baptized. And, you must continue to read the word of God daily! You must also pray daily as you are guided by the Holy Spirit. You must ask God for wisdom, knowledge, and for an understanding of His word, for the word of God is living and has power! Hebrews 4:12-13 says: For the word of God is quick and powerful and sharper than any two-edged sword, piercing even to the dividing asunder of the soul and spirit and the joints and marrow and is a discerner of the thoughts and intents of the heart; neither is there any creature that is not made known in his sight but all things are naked and opened unto the eyes of Him with whom we have to do. God is all-powerful, and all power belongs to God. God is all knowing because he knows all things and everything. God is also everywhere all the time at the same time! Proverbs 15:3 says: God's eyes are in every place looking at the good and evil. And when we do things, whether they are good or bad, God can see everything! And, we paid the consequences as a result of our actions. Isaiah 44:6 says: thus said the Lord, the King of Israel and His redeemer, the Lord of hosts, I am the first and I am the last, and besides me, there is no god. Isaiah 43:10 says: You are my witnesses, said the Lord, and my servant whom I have chosen, that you may know and believe me and understand that I am He. Before me, there was not god formed, neither shall there be after me! Isaiah 43:13 says: yes, before the day was I am He, and there is none that can deliver out of my hand. I will work who will let it. Before God stepped out into eternity, even before He said "Let there be light" and there was light, light came into being or began to exist by the power of God's word because it is and was God who spoke light into existence by the power of His word. God, Himself, is light! God made the day and the night; the light and the darkness are both alike God. Read Psalms 139:12. God is Almighty! God is and was before the heavens and the earth! God is in complete control of everything and all things and rightly so, because it is and was God who created everything and all things. Without God, we cannot do nothing. John 15:5 says: I am the vine. You are the branches. He that abides in me and I in him, the same brings forth much fruit, for without me, you cannot do nothing. For we move, live, and have our being because of God. God is great and His greatness is unsearchable. He is wonderful. How marvelous are His works and are past man's finding out. Ecclesiastes 3:11-14 says: God has made everything beautiful in His time. Also, he has set the world in their heart so that no man can find out the work that God made from the beginning to the end. I know that there is no good in them but for a man to rejoice and to do good in his life, and also, that every man should eat and drink and enjoy the good of his labor. It is the gift of God. I know that whatsoever God does, it shall be forever. Nothing can be put to it nor anything taken from it, and God does it that men should fear before Him. We can see the mighty works and power of God in a newborn baby, in the lofty, majestic mountains, in the valleys so low, in the different shapes and multitude of beautiful, colorful flowers, in the beautiful, blue sky and blanket of beautiful green grass, the rain, the snowflakes, the variety of trees, the rocks, the hills, streams, river, seas, the inventions of man (but man has to use something, which God has already created to make his inventions because only God can create). God is the past; God is the present; God is also the future. God is our shelter in the time of storm. We can live and abide in His care and lean upon His everlasting arms, arms that never fail. For God will never leave us nor forsake us. For the Lord said: teaching them to observe all things whatsoever I have commanded you, and lo, I am with you always, even unto the end of the world. Amen. We must trust completely in God, and we will receive the righteous desires of our heart, for Jesus Christ is our righteousness. We must love the Lord our God with all our heart, with all our soul, with all our mind, and with all our strength, and love our neighbor as ourselves. We must pray and read the word of God everyday, as we are guided by the Holy Spirit of God! We must ask God for wisdom, knowledge, and understanding, so that as we read and study the word of God daily, we will be able to understand His word and always apply it and use His word in our daily activities as we interact with others each day. We must put into practice the word of God in everything we do. This includes obeying God, according to His word and will, serving God by helping others, as we are led by the Holy Spirit. We must worship God in spirit and in truth. God is the only source of power. God is in complete control of everything because He is the final authority. He is eternity. He is infinite. Trust Him, and obey Him. Serve Him only. Seek God more than you look for precious gems, gold, jewels, silver, wealth, etc. for He is more precious than the finest of gold, silver, gems, jewels, wealth, relationships, and life, because in God and because of God, we have everlasting life, blessings, good health, and everlasting love, as well as everything else that we need and desire. Because when we delight ourselves in the Lord, He will give us the desires of our heart. Philippians 4:19-20 says: But my God shall supply all your needs according to His riches in glory by Christ Jesus. Now unto God our Father, be glory forever and ever. Amen. Everything belongs to God, for He has founded it upon the sea. He has established it upon the flood. Who shall ascend into the hill of the Lord, or who shall stand in His holy place? He that has clean hands and a pure heart, who has not lifted up his soul unto vanity nor sworn deceitfully. He shall receive the blessing from the Lord and righteousness from the God of his salvation. Praise you the Lord. The Lord is great and greatly to be praised, and His mercy endures forever to all generations. Praise God from whom all blessings flow.

Why and How Are We Created?

Thank God from whom all blessings flow. I greet you in the name of our Lord and Savior Jesus Christ and in the name of the Holy Spirit, our Comforter. The subject of this message is…Why and How Are We Created? We were and are created by the power of God Almighty! And, moreover, we are created for the glory of God! Isaiah 43:7 says: Even everyone that is called by my name: for I have created him for my glory: I have formed him, yes, I have made him. You are my witnesses says the Lord! And, my servant whom I have chosen, that you may know and believe me and understand that I am He: Before me, there was no god formed; neither shall there be after me! I even I am the Lord and beside me, there is no savior! For from everlasting to everlasting, I am God!

How did God create us? Genesis 2:7 says: And, the Lord God formed man from the dust of the ground and breathed into his nostrils the breath of life and man became a living soul! God is omnipotent, meaning He is all-powerful! God is omniscient because He knows everything and all things! God is omnipresent because he is everywhere all the time at the same time! God is the beginning and the ending! God is the source of all power! God is the first and the last! God is the Alpha and the Omega! For without God, we would not be or exist. "Be" is the most used verb in the English language. It is synonymous to I am. God said in Genesis 1:3: let there be light and there was light! And, so, light came to be and began to exist because of the power of God's word! God simply said "Let there be light" and the light appeared. Isn't that wonderful and amazing? The Almighty awesome power of God is far above our comprehension.

We cannot understand the power of God! God said in His word in Isaiah 55:8-9: for my thoughts are not your thoughts; neither are your ways my ways, says the Lord. For as the heavens are higher than the earth, so are my ways higher than your ways and my thoughts than your thoughts. No one can measure how far away heaven is from the earth. Scientist, astrologers, prognosticators, astronauts, etc., no one can measure the distance in relationship to how far heaven is from the earth. Only God knows and can measure the distance because the Bible plainly tells us that God knows everything and all things! For it is by the power of God that everything was made!

John, the writer of the fourth book of the four gospel books, chapter one, verses one through four: In the beginning was the word, and the word was with God, and the word was God! The same was in the beginning with God. All things were made by Him, and without Him was not anything made that was made. In Him was life, and the life was the light of men! And, so, it is the truth that God is the source of all power! God is the beginning and the ending. God is the first and the last. God Almighty is the Creator, who made the heavens and the earth! God is the essence of all things! For it is and was God who created and made all things. And, everything consists and exists because of God. Everything in heaven and in the earth does exist and is – because of God! The verb "is" is synonymous to the verb "be". Be is the same as I am. God referred to Himself as "I Am" when Moses asked God: "Who shall I say sent me?" when he went to Egypt to tell Pharaoh to let the children of Israel go. "I am" is in reference to God! It means "self-existent", which only applies to God! And, only God, Himself, can make that declaration because we live, move, and have our being because and by the power of God Almighty! Romans 13:1 says: Let every soul be subject unto the higher powers, for there is not power but of God. The powers that be are ordained of God! God is self-sufficient and independent! But, we are dependent upon God for all things. For, without God, we cannot do nothing. We live, move, and have our being because of God.

In life experiences or physics, there must be a cause before you can have an effect. The truth of the matter is that God is the cause and the effect. Because God is the Creator who created all things and everything, things visible and the things which are invisible! There are things that exist, which are invisible. The wind is invisible. We cannot see the wind, but we certainly can feel and see the physical effects of the wind. We can see the devastating effects of the wind in hurricanes or storms; how the trees are pulled up from the roots; tall buildings, houses, cars, trains, are lifted up from the earth. For God, Himself, rides upon the wings of the wind and makes the clouds His chariot. Because it is and was God who stretched out the north over the empty place and hang the earth upon nothing! God made the stars and put them in their place and called every star by name. God speaks to the lightnings, and the lightnings answer God by saying: Here we are!! What a mighty God we serve!

God speaks and a man will lay down and die, and God can speak again, and that very same man will get up and live again. I am reminded of Martha, the sister of Lazarus, who went to Jesus and said: "My brother Lazarus would not have died if you had been there. But, I know that even now, whatever you will ask of God, He will give it unto you!" Jesus said unto her: "Your brother will live again." Martha said: "I know that he will live again in the resurrection at the last day." Jesus said unto her: "I am the resurrection and the life! He that believes in me, though he were dead, yet shall he live again. And, whosoever lives and believes in me shall never die! Do you believe this?" She said unto Him: "Yes, Lord. I believe that you are Christ, the son of God, which should come into the world." And, Jesus went to the grave of Lazarus. Lazarus had been in the grave 4 days; his body had begun to decay, deteriorate, and stink. Jesus told them to take away the stone from the grave. Then, He lifted up His eyes and began to pray and said: "Father, I thank you that you have heard me already, and I know that You always hear me. But, because of the people which are standing by, I say it, that they may believe that you have sent me. And, after He had prayed to His Father in heaven, He cried with a loud voice: "Lazarus! Come forth!" And, Lazarus heard the voice of Jesus! The Anointed One! the Lamb of God! the Savior of the world! And, he got up and came out of the grave! He had on grave clothes and a napkin was wrapped around his face. Jesus said unto them: "Loose him, and let him go!" Lazarus was very much alive because sometime later, in the city of Bethany, Lazarus at supper with Jesus!

Jesus walks upon the sea and speaks to the sea and the wind! He said unto he sea and wind: "Peace, be still!" And, the billowing, strong waves of the sea became calm and still. The strong wind ceased and became calm.

Demons or whatever it be, they all shall obey His will! God made a path in the Red Sea, and the children of Israel walked across on dry land! He guided the children through the dry desert with fire by night, and during the day, He guided them by a cloud. He kept their enemies away from them. He protected them from the wild animals and snakes. He gave them water from a rock! And, we know, scientifically, it is impossible to get water from a rock. With man, this is impossible, but with God, all things are possible! Because it is impossible for God to fail! For God transcends time and space because God, Himself, is time! We are and were created by God for His glory!

We must work while it is day, while we still have time, and whatever we do must be done for the glory of God! WE must lift up the name of Jesus and He will draw all men unto Himself. Come to Jesus while you still have time. He will make your life brand new. And, He will save you from your sins. II Corinthians 5:17 says: therefore, if any man be in Christ, he is a new creature. Old things are passed away; behold all things are become new. But, God has commended His love toward us in that while we were yet sinners, Christ died for us. Salvation is a free gift given to us by God through His son Jesus Christ! Jesus Christ bought our salvation with His precious blood on the cross of Calvary. And, his blood will never lose its power! It flows to the highest mountain, and it flows to the lowest valley!

And, in my conclusion, I leave these words with you: the fields are white and the harvest is plenteous, but the laborers are few. And, so, let us get up out of our comfort zone and begin to do the work, which God has called us to do, as we are led by the Holy Spirit of God. And, whatever the Holy Spirit tells us to do, we must do all things for the glory of God. For we are and were created for the glory of God. Praise God from whom all blessings flow.

God Is My Defense

The subject of this message is: God is my defense. The scriptural text is Psalms 59:1-17. Defense is defined as having protection from opposition or trouble. I know beyond a shadow of a doubt that God is my defense. And, He will defend me! He will also protect me from all danger and harm or hurt because God is concerned about my welfare. God is truly able to fix and take care of all my problems, regardless of the severity of the situations. No one or nothing can come near or against me because of God's presence. Because God is all-powerful, and He is everywhere all the time at the same time. And, God knows everything and all things. And, He is able to do exceedingly, abundantly above all that we can ask or think according to the power that works in us. For God called those things that be not as though they were. In the beginning, God created the heaven and the earth. And God said: Let there be light, and there was light! And, by the power of God's word, light began to exist. Hebrews 4:12 says: for the word of God is quick and powerful and sharper than any two-edged sword, piercing even to the dividing asunder of the soul and spirit and of the joints and marrow and is a discerner of the thoughts and intents of the heart. It is the truth that God is the beginning and the ending. God is the first and the last. "Be" is a derivative of I am, for it is and was I Am, who is God, who said: "Let there be…" And, whatever God said "Let there be.." came to be and began to exist because of the power of God's word! God knows the ending at the beginning because God is the beginning.

God is the beginning; God is the source of all power! Romans 13:1 says: Let every soul be subject unto the higher powers, for there is no power but of God; the powers that be are ordained of God! Isaiah 43:10 says: you are my witnesses, said the Lord, and my servant whom I have chosen that you may know and believe me and understand that I am he. Before me, there was no god formed, neither shall there be after me. For from everlasting to everlasting, God is God. And, God will always be God! And, only God can create because God is and was before nothing! What is nothing? Nothing does not exist. God is the source of all power! God is the very essence and fiber of our being, for truly we live, move, and have our being because of God! Without God, we would not and can not exist. Everything exists or came into existence because of God.

God's word is living and has power! God and His word are synonymous. God is His word, and His word is God. John 1:1 says: In the beginning was the word, and the word was with God, and the word was God. And, so, I know that God is my defense and He will defend me regardless of the circumstances or situations, for God's grace is sufficient for any and every situation, regardless of the severity of the circumstance. We must look beyond the circumstance and see Jesus, who is the author and finisher of our faith. We must have steadfast and abiding, unmoveable faith, which will move mountains. Jesus said unto his disciples: Have faith in God, for truly, I say unto you that whosoever shall say unto this mountain: "Be you removed and be cast into the sea" and shall not doubt in his heart but shall believe that those things which he said shall come to pass, he shall have whatsoever he said. Therefore, I say unto you what things soever you desire, when you pray, believe that you received them, and you shall have them.

As I was reading in the Psalms, God gave me that kind of faith! And, because of the faith which God has given to me, I am truly blessed. I know that God will answer my prayer and the prayers of faithful Christians. God is infinite! God is from everlasting to everlasting! God is eternal and eternity! And, God is forever! Moreover, God knows everything and all things! Because it is and was God who created and made all things by the power of His word! In Genesis the first chapter, verse one: In the beginning, God created the heaven and the earth! God is wonderful and most worthy of all praise and thanksgiving. Let everything that has breath praise you the Lord for His mighty acts and wonderful works! For he is gracious and full of compassion, slow to anger and of great mercy. God is good to all of us. And, His mercies are over all His works. For the Lord is great and greatly to be praised. And, His greatness is unsearchable! God is our deliverer. God is our salvation. God is our refuge. God is our help in the time of need and trouble. God is our shelter in the storms of life. When our family and our friends forget about us, God will never leave us nor forsake us! God is the same yesterday, today, and forever more. Weeping may endure for a night, but joy comes in the morning. I have had many trials and tribulations. I have been through the storms of life. But, by the grace of God, I made it over. Trust God, and never doubt. For God will bring us through the flood, the rain, and the storms of life. And God will place our feet on higher ground. God is our defense in any situation or circumstance. In the courtroom, He is our judge, our jury, and our lawyer. And, He has never lost a case! He is our doctor in a sick room, and God has never lost a patient! God feeds us when we are hungry. God gives us water when we are thirsty. God, in the days of Moses, made water come from a rock, and the children of Israel drank water from that rock. God made an ax float on the water. God spoke to Moses from a burning bush. God spoke to Job from a whirlwind. God speaks to the lightnings, and the lightnings answer God by saying: Here we are. God parted the Red Sea, and the Israelites walked on dry land in the middle of the sea. What a mighty God we serve! God walks upon the wind, and God makes even the clouds His chariot. God can see the earth form heaven. We cannot see the future. We cannot see through dark clouds. But, we know God holds the future. We also know that it is God who holds our hands.

    We must walk on by faith each day. On a Monday, on a Tuesday, on a Wednesday, on a Thursday, on a Friday, on a Saturday, and on a Sunday, walk on by faith in God. God is always listening to our prayers, and He will answer. That divorce you are going through; that relative who is on drugs; those loved ones who you just cannot seem to reach; and you have been waiting for a financial blessing. Your children are out of control. Your husband or wife is on the verge of leaving. You are left home alone with sick loved ones who you are very concerned about, and no one cares, but God cares, and God specializes in things that are impossible. For with God, all things are possible! God is our defense, and He will defend us. I don't worry; I don't fret because God cannot fail, and He never fails. Just keep the faith, and never cease to pray. Walk upright morning, noon, and night because He will be there. He is right on time because God, Himself, is time. And, without God, there would not be time because God transcends time and space. God, Himself, is time and space.

And, in my conclusion, I leave these words with you: We must have complete faith in God Almighty. It is the truth that because of God's presence and power, we are victorious and successful in all of our efforts and endeavors. We must acknowledge God in all our ways, and God will, beyond a shadow of a doubt, direct our path. We must trust in God with all of our heart and lean not unto our own understanding, and God will direct our path. We must ask God for directions, wisdom, and instructions. And, He will help us. If I don't see you anymore or talk to you again, walk on by faith in God. Praise God from whom *all* blessings flow!

A Place Called Hell

Thanking God Almighty, who is the Father of our Lord and Savior Jesus Christ, the sender of the Holy Spirit, who is our Comforter. It is by the mercy of God and by His power that I am here today to share with you this message, which God, in His infinite wisdom and power, has helped me to prepare for your hearing and admonition. And, to encourage you with the word of God! This message is a very deep, serious and sobering, thought-provoking message. Please listen carefully to this message. The subject of this message is a placed called hell. What is hell? Hell is s a place of eternal punishment. (Matthew 25:46; Revelation 14:10-11; Luke 16:19-31) Hell is described as a place of torment and punishment, a place of outer darkness, where no one outside of hell can ever come to you, and you can never leave or get out of hell. If you go there, you will be there forever, tormented by the burning eternal flames of hell. You will remain there for all eternity. You will not be able to call on God or come before the presence of God. This place called hell is prepared for the devil and his angels. (Read Matthew chapter 25, verse 41). And, for the beast, false prophets, and the worshippers of the beast, (read Revelation chapter 19, verse 20), and for those who have rejected Jesus Christ, the savior of the world, and the gospel. Hell is for those who are liars, sinners, and for those who have not asked God to forgive them for their sins; those who have not accepted Jesus Christ as their Lord and Savior; and those who do not obey God and His word. It is also for those who do not know Jesus Christ as their personal savior. Those are the ones who will be there in hell. We know that there is a heaven, and there is also a hell. Heaven is the place where God lives, where there is love, joy, peace, Christ Jesus, and the Holy Spirit. The glory of God is in heaven. Revelation 19:1 says…And, after these things, I heard a great voice of much people in heaven singing Alleluia, salvation and glory and honor and power unto the Lord our God! Revelation 21:22-27: And, I saw no temple therein, for the Lord God Almighty and the Lamb are the temple of it. And, the city had no need of the sun, neither the moon to shine in it for the glory of God did lighten it, and the Lamb is the light thereof. And, the nations of them which are saved, shall walk in the light of it. And, the kings of the earth do bring their glory and honor into it. And, the gates of it shall not be shut at all by day for there shall be no night there. And, they shall bring the glory and honor of the nations into it. And, there shall in no wise enter into it anything that defileth, neither whatsoever worketh abomination or maketh a lie: but they which are written in the Lamb's book of life. Revelation 22:1-7, 11-13 says…And, he shewed me a pure river of water of life, clear as crystal, proceeding out of the throne of God and the Lamb. In the midst of the street of it, and on either side of the river, was there the tree of life, which bare twelve manner of fruits and yielded her fruit every month: and the leaves of the tree were for the healing of the nations. And, there shall be no more curse: but the throne of God and of the Lamb shall be in it, and his servants shall serve Him. And, they shall see His face; and His name shall be in their foreheads, and there shall be no night there; and they need no candle, neither light of the sun for the Lord God giveth them light: and they shall reign forever and ever. And he said unto me, these sayings are faithful and true; and the Lord God of the holy prophets sent his angel to shew unto his servants the things which must shortly be done. Behold, I come quickly: blessed is he that keepeth the saying of the prophecy of this book. He that is unjust, let him be unjust still: and he which is filthy, let him be filthy still: and he that is righteous, let him be righteous still: and he that is holy, let him be holy still. And, behold, I come quickly; and my reward is with me to give every man according as his work shall be. I am Alpha and Omega, the beginning and the end, the First and the Last.

Those of us who have heard and read the word of God and have asked God to forgive us for our sins and have believed that Jesus Christ is the only begotten son of God and that He died for our sins and that He rose again the third day and He is now at the right hand of God, making intercession for us. I Corinthians 15:34 says: For I delivered unto you, first of all, that which I also received, how that Christ died for our sins according to the scriptures, and He was buried and rose again the third day according to the scriptures. As Christians, we must read the word of God everyday as we are guided by the Holy Spirit. We must also pray everyday and ask God to guide us and help us to do those things, which He has called us to do each day. We must rely on God for wisdom, knowledge, understanding, and strength because without God, we cannot do nothing. Because we are totally dependent on God for everything. Because God is the one who created us, and we move, live, and have our being in God. God is the very essence and fiber of our life. Because it is and was God who gave us life. And, it is essential that we know God, the Holy Spirit, and Jesus Christ as our personal savior. And, He must be the lord of our life, in that we obey Him and follow His example. For Jesus Christ is the one and only example or role model, which we must follow in order to be right in everything we do or say. We must read the word of God everyday as we are guided by the Holy Spirit. We must <u>not</u> try to interpret the word of God, and we should not accept the interpretation of others because II Peter chapter one, verses twenty and twenty-one say: knowing this first, that no prophecy of the scripture is of any private interpretation. For the prophecy came not in old time by the will of man; but holy men of God spake as they were moved by the Holy Spirit. And, so, we must be directed by God and listen to God's Holy Spirit as we read the word of God. We must obey the word of God as we are guided by the Holy Spirit of God. We must submit ourselves completely unto the will of God. We must share the word of God with others as we are guided and directed by the Holy Spirit of God. It is important that we know God and His word because if we do not know God and His word, how can we tell others about god and His word? We must praise and thank God each day, as we are guided by the Holy Spirit. For God is most worthy of all praise and thanksgiving. For God is great and greatly to be praised, and His greatness is unsearchable. How marvelous are His works. Ecclesiastes 3:14 says: He has made everything beautiful in His time; also he has set the world in their heart, so that no man can find out the work that God maketh from the beginning to the end. I know that whatsoever God does, it shall be forever. Nothing can be put to it, nor anything taken from it, and God does it that men should fear before Him. We must thank and praise God for eternal life, for His mercy that endures forever, for His amazing grace that is sufficient for any and every situation, for His multitude of blessings, with which He blesses us daily, moment by moment; for

His healing power, protection, joy, peace, and for His everlasting love with which he loves us. Jeremiah 31:3 says: The Lord has appeared of old unto me, saying, yes, I have loved you with an everlasting love; therefore, with lovingkindness, have I drawn you. John 3:16 says: For God so loved the world that He gave his only begotten son that whosoever believes in Him should not perish but have everlasting life! We must not look at the circumstances, but look above and beyond the circumstances and see Jesus! Because Jesus can and He will fix it for us.

He fixed it for Lazarus who was indeed dead because He had been in the grave buried for four days. Jesus, the matchless Lamb of God, came to the grave of Lazarus. He told them to roll away the stone from the grave, and Jesus lifted up His voice and said: Father, I thank you that you have heard me already. And, I know that you hear me always, but because of the people who are standing by, I say it, that they may believe that you have sent me. And, when He thus had spoken, He cried with a loud voice: Lazarus come forth! And, Lazarus, who was indeed dead, heard the voice of Jesus, and he got up and came out of the grave. He was wrapped up in grave clothes and a napkin was wrapped over his face. And, it covered his face. Jesus said unto them: Loose him, and let him go! He was alive and well because some time later, he (Lazarus) ate dinner with Jesus in the city of Bethany. Jesus is resurrection power! Jesus is deliverance power! Jesus is healing power! Jesus is eternal life! Jesus is water in dry places. Jesus is the bread of life. Jesus is the water of life. Jesus is my shelter in the time of storm. Jesus is my doctor in intensive care. He moves from intensive care to complete recovery. He is my judge, lawyer, jury in any courtroom. He is the bright and morning star. Jesus is the rose or Sharon. He is the light of the world and is forever shining in my soul. And, so, I will walk in the light, beautiful light because this light shines all around me by day and by night. Because in Jesus, there is no darkness. The light and the darkness are both alike to Jesus.

Elijah did not die. He went up into heaven in a chariot of fire and horses of fire because he trusted and obeyed God. Enoch was a man of faith, and he walked with God. He went up into heaven whole – soul and body. Job endured for righteousness. He had sores, boils from the top of his head to the soles of his feet. He suffered and lost everything including his children. But, Job continued to pray and trust in God during his illness. Job said: I know my Redeemer lives and though after my skin worms destroy this body, yet in my flesh will I see God! Jeremiah was put in a deep dungeon with mud above his waist. He had to be let down by a rope into the dungeon. He was put there because he preached the word of God. He said the word of God is just like fire shut up in my bones. Peter and the apostles were beaten and put in jail because they preached the gospel. Peter said: We ought to obey God rather than man. As servants of God, we must teach and preach the word of God as we are guided by the Holy Spirit of God. We must continue, even in the midst of persecution.

Believe me when I tell you, you do not want to go to hell. It is a place of eternal torment, punishment, and outer darkness. It is a lake of fire and flames, a place where all the wicked are, where the beast and the false prophets, worshippers of Satan, the devil and for those

WHO IS GOD?

who will not ask God to forgive them for their sins, those who do not accept Jesus Christ as their Lord and Savior. Make no mistake: this fire and flame can be felt bodily. You will have your memory. You cannot leave or escape. You will feel the intense heat of the fire and flames, and you will burn forever. So, make that decision today, right now! Come to Jesus while you have time. He will make your life brand new, and He will take care of you. He will forgive you for your sins, and He will save you. And, so, when you pray and ask God to forgive you for your sins, you must accept Jesus Christ as your personal Lord and Savior. Additionally, you must know God and His word. You must obey God and His word as you are guided by the Holy Spirit of God. In order to know God and His word, it is necessary to prayerfully read the word of God daily, asking God to give you wisdom, knowledge, and understanding of His word. You must also submit yourself totally unto the will of God. We must know God and His word. We must also obey God and His word. It is also necessary to share the word of God with others as we are guided and directed by the Holy Spirit of God. We must be cognizant of God's eternal presence, for God is everywhere all the time at the same time. For God transcends time and space because God, Himself, is time. Without God, there would not be time. But, because of God, we have time. God is all-powerful. God created the heavens and the earth by the power of His word. Whatever God said "Let there be" came into existence by the power of God's word. God is great, and His greatness is unsearchable. O Lord our Lord how excellent is your name in all the earth. And, in my conclusion, if you have accepted Jesus as your Savior and Lord, you will not go to hell. And, if you have not personally asked God to forgive you for your sins, please do so today, for tomorrow may be too late. May God bless you eternally. Praise God from whom all blessings flow.

Power In The Word of God

Thanking God, from whom all blessings flow; the subject of this message is: Power in the Word of God! The scriptural text is from Matthew, the twenty-eighth chapter, verses 1-20. Truly, there is power in the word of God Almighty! For God is the beginning and the ending. God is the first and the Last. The truth of the matter is: God is and was before nothing. What is nothing? Nothing does not exist. God has always been. God is now. And, God will always be. For from everlasting to everlasting, God is God. God is the beginning and the source of all power! Romans 13:1 says: Let every soul be subject unto the higher powers. For there is no power but of God: the powers that be are ordained of God. God is the one and only true and living eternal God! For it is and was God who created the heavens and the earth by the power of His word. And, God said: "Let there be light" and there was light. And, so, it is the truth that light came to be or began to exist by the power of God's word. Isaiah 44:24 says: Thus said the Lord, your Redeemer, and He that formed you from the womb, I am the Lord that makes all things, that stretches forth the heavens alone, that spread abroad the earth by myself. Hebrews 11:3 says: Through faith, we understand that the worlds were framed by the word of God, so that things which are seen were not made of things which do appear. Isaiah 43:10 says: you are my witnesses said the Lord and my servants whom I have chosen; that you may know and believe me and understand that I am He; before me there was not god formed, neither shall there be after me. John 1:1 says: In the beginning was the Word, and the Word was with God, and the Word was God. The same was in the beginning with God. All things were made by Him, and without Him was not anything made that was made. In Him was life and the life was the light of men.

God is all-powerful. God knows everything and all things. God is everywhere all the time at the same time. God never slumbers or sleeps. God can speak to the lightnings, and the lightnings answer God by saying "Here we are". Just imagine the lightnings speaking to God. What an awesome, all-powerful, infinite, eternal, wonderful, great God, and His greatness is unsearchable. He is the most high God. How marvelous are all His works, which He created by the power of His word. How excellent is His name in all the earth! Let everything that has breath praise you the Lord! God is most worthy of all praises and thanksgiving. We must make a joyful noise unto the Lord! We must come before His presence with singing. The Lord is good, and His mercy endures forever, to all generations. Because His mercies are new every morning and everyday. And, all we have needed, God has already provided. Great is the Lord's faithfulness. And, we must be faithful in doing the work which God has called us to do. We must be faithful in the reading of God's word. We must obey God and His word. And, we must also share the word of God with others as we are guided by the Holy Spirit of God. We must pray everyday as well as during / throughout the day and at night as well as during / throughout the night. I Thessalonians 5:17 says: Pray without ceasing. Luke 18:1 says: And He spoke a parable unto them to this end; that men ought to always pray and not faint.

We must seek first the kingdom of God and His righteousness, and all these other things will be added unto us. It is very necessary to trust in the Lord with all our hearts and lean not upon our own understanding but in all our ways acknowledge God, and He will direct our path. We must keep our minds stayed on the Lord for He will keep us in perfect peace when our minds are always on God. We must be faithful and steadfast, always doing the work of the Lord Jesus Christ, knowing that only what we do for Christ will last. (Matthew 25:35-46; Psalms 82:3-4) We must visit those who are sick and those who are in prison, and we must help the poor and needy. We must have love and compassion for others.

For God so loved the world that He gave His only begotten son, that whosoever believes in Him shall not perish but shall have everlasting life. Because God is love. And, He loves us with an everlasting love. We can take our cares and concerns to God, and He will solve them, regardless of the severity of the situations or circumstances. We must look beyond the circumstances and see Jesus. Because Jesus never fails. Jesus is able to do exceeding abundantly above all that we can ask or think according to the power that works in us. That power is the Holy Spirit of God, which is in us, those of us who are believers and followers of Jesus Christ – Jesus Christ, the righteous, who is our Lord and Savior.

The word of God is quick and powerful and sharper than any two-edged sword, penetrating even to the dividing asunder of the soul and of the spirit and of the joints and marrow and is a discerner of the thoughts and intents of the heart. God knows our thoughts even before they come into our minds. God knew that we would be doing what we are doing at this very moment. God knew this even before He created the heaven and the earth. For it is and was God who created everything and all things by the power of His word! Whatever God said "Let there be.." came to be and began to exist because of the power of God's word! God is synonymous to His word. God is His word. His word is God. Isaiah 40:8 says: the grass will wither, and the flower will fade, but the word of God will stand forever! Psalms 119:89 says: Forever O' Lord, your word is settled in heaven. Through faith, we understand that the worlds were framed by the word of God, so that things which are seen, were not made of things which do appear.

Genesis 1:1 says: In the beginning God created the heaven and the earth! And, so, based on this biblical truth, we know and understand (because of the wisdom God has given to us). For without wisdom from God, we would not have understanding nor would we have the ability to learn or acquire knowledge. Because the wisdom of God gives us the ability to learn and get knowledge and understanding. Because wisdom is knowledge guided by understanding, which only God can give to us.

Did you know that the word of God is living and has power? God can speak, and a man will lay down and die. God can speak again and that same man will get up and live again, because of the word of God. Lazarus died and was buried and He was in the grave for four days. But, Jesus, the Word of God, came to the grave of Lazarus. He told them to take away the stone from the grave, and they took away the stone. And, Jesus, the Lamb of God, lifted up His eyes and said: Father, I thank you that you have heard me already. And, I know that you always hear me, but because of the people who are standing by, I say it, that they may believe that you have sent me. And, when He thus had spoken, He cried with a loud voice: Lazarus, come forth! And, Lazarus, who was indeed dead, heard the voice of Jesus, and he came out of the grave. He was wrapped up, hands and feet, with grave clothes and his face was covered and wrapped with a napkin. Jesus said unto them: Loose him, and let him go! He was alive and well because some time later, he (Lazarus) ate dinner with Jesus in the city of Bethany. God spoke to Job from a whirlwind. God spoke to Moses from a burning bush. God spoke to Jonah in the belly of a whale. God speaks to the strong waves of the sea, and they become calm and still. God speaks to the lightning, and the lightning ceases to flash across the sky. God speaks to the demons, and they obey Him. Whatever it be, they shall all obey the will of God Almighty, the one and only Creator; the only true, living and eternal God. God is infinite. God is eternity. God knows the ending at the beginning. God is the First and the Last. God is sovereign. God is in complete control of everything and all things! The word of God will stand forever. Praise God from whom all blessings flow.

A Possible God In An Impossible Situation

The subject of this message is: "A Possible God In An Impossible Situation". This message was inspired and directed by God, Christ, and the Holy Spirit and is very profound and not of a pragmatic nature. Because with God, all things are possible! For God is the beginning and the ending. God is the First and the Last. God is he source of all power! Without God, we can do nothing! But, through Christ, which is the power of God – the Holy Spirit is also the power of God – we can do all things. God is and was before nothing. What is nothing? Nothing does not exist. But, God is all-powerful and God knows everything and all things. God is everywhere all the time at the same time! God is self-existent. We must depend on God for everything, including life! For, without God, we could not inhale and exhale, nor could we wake up or awake every morning without the power of God! For God calls those things that be not as though they were! And, with God's power and His directions, we can do all things through Christ. We can do these things because of our faith in God and with the Holy Spirit, which is the power of God that is in us. These things are made possible.

Jesus healed all kind of diseases and illnesses and sickness with the power of His word and sometimes with just a touch or at other times, even when others touched the hem of his garment, they were immediately healed and made whole, like the woman who had a bleeding disorder or disease! She had been to many doctors and had spent all of her money on doctor bills. She did not get any better but in fact, she grew worse. But, one day, when Jesus was passing by, as feeble and as weak as she was, she pressed her way through the crowd of people. And, she said if I can just touch the hem of the garment of Jesus, I will be healed and made whole! And, she reached out and touched just the hem of the garment of Jesus, and immediately, she was healed and made whole! The bleeding stopped! God and Jesus gave His disciples power to heal all kinds of diseases and sickness. I am reminded of the incident of the man who was born crippled. And, he had never been able to walk. This man was carried by others, and they laid him at the gate of the temple. And, as people went into the temple to pray and worship God, the crippled man would ask for money. One day, Peter and John were going to the temple at the hour of prayer. The crippled man asked them for some money, and Peter looked at the man who was crippled and said unto him: "Look at us!" And, the crippled man looked at them, expecting to receive something from them. And, Peter said unto him: "I don't have any silver or gold, but such as I have, I give unto you. In the name of Jesus of Nazareth, get up and walk!" And, because of the name of Jesus, the crippled man not only got up, but he jumped up and ran into the temple, running and praising God!! God's miracles and healing power are very prevalent and alive today! When we have complete faith in God and obey Him and His word, healing and miracles are done. Marriages are healed and reconciled. Families come together in peace and love. Neighborhood relationships are improved. Management and employees are more cooperative. School situations become less dangerous and more manageable. Children are less rebellious and more obedient. For God is the answer, and God has the solution for all of our problems and situations! When we pray with complete faith in God, as we are guided by the Holy Spirit of God, God will hear us and He will answer our prayers! But, we must know God and His word. We must also obey God and His word! We must seek you first the kingdom of God and His righteousness and all these other things will be added unto us. We must trust in the Lord with all our heart and lean not unto our own understanding, but in all of our ways, acknowledge God, and He will direct our path. We must delight ourselves in the Lord, and He will give us the desires of our heart. We must be steadfast, unmoveable, always abounding in the work of the Lord; forasmuch as we know that our labor in the Lord is not in vain. And, so, we must be faithful and consistent in obeying God and His word. He will give us a crown of life (Revelation 2:10). Because God specializes in things that are impossible. Matthew 19:26 says: But Jesus beheld them and said unto them, with men, this is impossible, but with God, all things are possible. Because God cannot fail! It is the truth that God calls those things that be not as though they were! It is and was God who created the heavens and the earth by the power of His word! And, so, because God is all-powerful! And, God knows everything and all things! God is also everywhere all the time at the same time because God, Himself, is time!

And, so, in my conclusion, I know that God can do the impossible! Because with God, all things are possible! Jeremiah 32:17 says: Ah Lord God, behold you have made the heaven and the earth by your great power and stretched out arms and there is nothing too hard for God! Praise God from whom all blessings flow.

Workshops

How To Help Hurting People

First of all, we must determine the causation or what precedes the problem. There are many different kinds of hurts. Some people's hurts stem from early childhood and carry over into adulthood. For example, some children are abused, and as a result of being abused as a child, they themselves become abusive. Or, in the case of when little or no love or affection is shown in a household, it affects especially the children who are exposed to this kind of environment. This kind of action and treatment has a negative effect in regards to the behavior of the children raised in such an environment. Almost, inevitably, they will acquire and practice the same type of behavior.

Now, let us look at the flipside of the coin. In a home where true love and affection is demonstrated in a Godly way, the end result is contrary to the first analogy. It is as different as night and day because it is so far removed from the first example, e.g. when Godly love is practiced in a home, sibling from this home are usually good-natured and easy to get along with. They are willing to share and compromise and forgive, whereas type A are not willing to forgive. Moreover, they blame others for their mistakes and shortcomings. As a matter of fact, they try to justify their mistakes by blaming others for their mistakes and they become takers instead of givers. As a rule, they couldn't care less when some one is the recipient of abusiveness or vindictiveness. It is very rare for type A to even offer an apology when they have hurt some one. They are too self-centered or arrogant to say "I was wrong; please forgive me" or "I'm sorry". On the other hand, type B is usually careful not to hurt others. And, when they do, it is not done deliberately or purposely. And, when this type of action occurs, type B will become very penitent, remorseful, and will do whatever is necessary or needful to rectify, change, or correct the situation. We will explore, more in detail, the problems of hurting people. We will also look at possible solutions.

There are hurting people throughout the universe, and the ramification of hurts are extremely devastating and are most prevalent among all nations. There are many kinds of hurts; at this point, we shall list a few. However, time and space will not permit us to list them all e.g. some people are hurting because of illness, homelessness, abusiveness by sex offender, wife beaters, rapists; world hunger, drugs, unfair treatment of bureaucrats, broken homes, divorce, separation, loneliness, hopelessness, depression, stress, fear, hatred, gang violence, liars, crime, murders, prejudice, inequality, which has many facets. In order to cover all of the hurts and ills of the world, we would need more pages than I care to write or am able to cover or include in the time allowed of this particular session. The aforementioned list of hurts can be and will be eradicated and will become non-existent when Christ shall come to claim His own elect, those who are called according to His purpose; those who have heard the gospel of God and Christ, which is the good news of the kingdom of God and Christ, where God and Christ are the rulers in this kingdom. It is a kingdom of peace, righteousness, and joy in the Holy Ghost or Holy Spirit. When you hear the gospel or word of God, you must believe the gospel and repent and accept Jesus Christ as your personal savior. Salvation is a personal commitment. You must confess with your mouth and believe in your heart that Jesus died for your sins, for it is the truth that Jesus died for the sins of the whole world. John 3:16 says: For God so loved the world that He gave His only begotten son that whosoever believes in Him should not perish but have everlasting life. We cannot buy or pay for salvation or eternal life. Because our Lord and Savior Jesus Christ paid for our salvation with His precious blood. For His blood will never lose its power! For Jesus is the eternal sacrifice for sin. He offered up His life once and for all (a sacrifice for sin by the which we are sanctified through the offering of the body of Jesus Christ once and for all). Hebrews 10:10 We must love the Lord our God as stated in Luke 10:27 (And he answering said, thou shall love the Lord thy God with all thy heart and with all thy soul, and with all thy strength and with all thy mind and thy neighbor as thyself.) Let us, at this point in time, consider carefully and prayerfully this particular passage of scripture. These are indeed the very words of Jesus, the Son of God, and our Savior! And, whatever Jesus said or taught came directly from God, our Heavenly Father. These are living words. These words are life; these words are everlasting; these words are infinite; these are the very words of God!

It is very necessary that we do precisely what God tells us to do in His spoken and written word, for Christ came to do the will and work of His Father in heaven. (Please read John 14:9-31; John 10:30-41 for references.) People are hurting because of racial prejudice and social injustice; discrimination in job opportunities and housing; not being accepted into various organizations, agencies and clubs that exist throughout the world. People are hurting because there is little or no integrity or concern demonstrated or shown by politicians and/or bureaucrats in regards to the public or people they allegedly serve and protect. They procrastinate and promise you much, but in actuality, you get little or nothing! People are hurting because they feel that there is no hope for survival or deliverance from painful and stressful situations that plague our societies of today; broken homes, broken promises, illegal schemes and scams practiced and used by some professionals and by non-professionals; deception in business ventures and sales, health care, home repairs, just to name a few. They are deeply involved in get rich quick schemes and scams. Various agencies and corporations have become corrupt. Governments are decaying and crumbling. Child molestation and child abuse has become more prevalent and obvious. Sex offenses and homosexuality is blatant and is on the increase. Cheating, lying, embezzling is at an all time high within the framework of our governments. And, this deception is worldwide. Millions of people are affected in a negative manner and are hurting because of these grave and devastating conditions imposed upon us because of the irresponsibility and lack of accountability being practiced within the halls of justice. Broken homes, broken relationships are more prevalent, and it is because of the lack of the love of God being demonstrated from the heart, as we interact with one another. Nor do we put into practice and use the wisdom which comes only from God! We tend to rely on human intellect or man's wisdom. We hurt because we do not have complete abiding faith in God. We hurt because we do not have accurate knowledge of God, nor do we have the patience and the necessary understanding or insight into the word of God. We fail to show real concern for others duties or obligations which God instructs us to do by way of His word, found in the

Holy Bible, which is our solemn duty and responsibility to obey and follow. It is essential that we prayerfully, meditatively read the word of God on a daily basis, asking God to give us wisdom, knowledge, and an understanding of His word. Additionally, we must know God and His word. We must also obey and share the word with others in the power of God's Holy Spirit. In so doing, we will not be guilty of trying to interpret the word ourselves. Neither should we use the interpretation of others. We must rely solely and completely on God, Christ, and the Holy Spirit, the one universal interpretation of the word of God! II Peter 1:20-21 says: (knowing this first, that no prophecy of the scripture is of any private interpretation). II Timothy 3:16 says: all scripture is given by inspiration of God, and is profitable for doctrine, for reproof, for correction, for instruction in righteousness. When we know the instructions and principles of God and apply them in our daily involvements as we interact with others in unity, people who are hurting will be healed. The reason our societies are plagued with so many ills and problems is because we do not know God and His word, nor do we obey His word. As the saying goes: for every action, there is a reaction. We find in the book of Deuteronomy the 28th chapter, when the Israelites were obedient to the word of God, they were abundantly blessed because of their obedience to God. On the other hand, when they were disobedient, they were plagued by various curses because of their wrongdoings or disobedience. God is love. He is also good and merciful to all of us. He blesses us moment by moment, and day by day. Many of His precious and wonderful blessings, which he bestows upon each of us universally; we sometimes take those blessings and gifts for granted. There are times when we take for granted or assume that we will wake up in the morning. But, when we awake and get up each morning, it is a gift from God; the gift of life and one more day that God has given us, not because of who we are or that we deserve it, but it is because of who He is and because He is merciful. And, His compassions fail not. Morning by morning, new mercies we see; all that we have needed, God has provided. Great is his faithfulness to us. He is a loving Father to us all. We often suffer needlessly because we fail to follow and obey the instructions of our Heavenly Father. Psalms 84:11 says: For the Lord God is a sun and shield! The Lord will give grace and glory: no good thing will He withhold from them that walk upright. When we know and obey the instructions of God, we will grow spiritually and prosper and be healthy. For, in God and Christ, we are complete physically, spiritually, and mentally. We forfeit many blessings from God when we are disobedient to God. We experience many misfortunes and suffer needless pains because we fail to obey God and His word. There is hope! There are solutions to every problem facing today's world. The solution being that we must put our hurts and our problems into the capable hands of God Almighty who has the only solution to all of our hurts and problems. He can and will also solve all of our problems and will heal our hurts, regardless of the severity of the situation. But, we must ask, and when we ask, we must exercise complete, unmoveable, abiding faith in God, not doubting or wavering. We must cast all of our cares upon God because God loves us and He cares. He is concerned about our every need. Philippians 4:19 says: but my God shall supply all your needs according to His riches in glory by Christ Jesus. We must learn to be still and know that our Heavenly Father is God and besides Him, there is no god. We must stand still and see the salvation and deliverance of God Almighty. For the battle is not ours, but the battle is the Lord's. Nothing is too hard for God; for with God, all things are possible. We must pray as we are led by the Holy Spirit of God. We must follow the example of Christ, our Savior, for He is the only role model that we must follow. But, we must know who He is, how He lived, and how He walked. It is most essential that we know Christ's example. And, we must also follow His example. We can find the lifestyle of Jesus, our Savior, within the pages of the Holy Bible, which is the infallible, inerrant word of God. For God is the author of the Bible, even though He chose certain writers to pen the Bible. They wrote as they were moved by God's Holy Spirit. (Please read II Peter 1:20-21 for references.) We must become actively involved in the work of God, by helping those in need. There are countless needs that we can attend to, e.g. We can help by reading to some one who is unable to read, visiting nursing homes, volunteering in a hospital, visiting the sick and shut-in, becoming involved in the needs of your community, helping the homeless, giving to some needy person, etc. There are many children as well as adults who don't have proper food or clothing. You can go to the store for some elderly or handicapped person. You can be a witness for Christ and God by sharing the word of God as you are directed by the Holy Spirit, for it is necessary to acknowledge God in all of our ways and endeavors. And, He will guide us. When He is guiding us, we are assured of success and safety. We must trust God completely and rely on Him for all things; instructions, guidance, or whatever our needs are, God will supply them. It is His will that we are healthy and that we are prosperous, and He will give us the desires of our hearts, when we delight ourselves in Him by obeying Him according to His will. Sometimes, we hinder or prevent our blessing when we are disobedient to God. And, so, let us draw close and near to God. (Submit yourselves therefore unto God. Resist the devil, and He will flee from you. – James 4:7) The problems and illnesses of the world can and will be resolved when God is in control of our lives. We must obey and serve God only as He guides and instructs us. Happy are the people that trust in God. And, righteous are the people that obey and follow the instructions of God. God will heal our hurts and illnesses if we follow His instructions. II Chronicles 7:14 says: If my people who are called by my name shall humble themselves and pray and seek my face, and turn from their wicked ways, then will I hear from heaven and will forgive their sins and will heal their land. We must seek ye first the kingdom of God and His righteousness and all these things shall be added unto you. Praise ye the Lord! If we obey and serve God only, He will heal us and make us whole and complete. For Christ died for our total healing. When we obey and serve God to the fullest, He will heal our hurts. Weeping may endure for a night but joy comes in the morning. And, in the morning, we will hurt no more. Thanks be to God who gives us the victory through our Lord Jesus Christ. Praise ye the Lord. There is nothing too hard for God, for all things are possible with God, for there is no failure in God! Philippians 4:13 says: I can do all things through Christ who strengthens me.

Let us keep in mind Romans 8:37-39, and I Corinthians 15:58. (Please read the above scriptures for edification.) I pray that God Almighty will abundantly bless all who read this book. Praise God from whom all blessings flow.

Faith and Stewardship Go Hand in Hand

Faith is complete trust and belief in God, Christ, and the Holy Spirit. (John 14:1, 15, 17, & 26) Faith is a gift given to us by God. We, the believers, believe in God, Christ, and the Holy Spirit through the word of God, found in the Holy Scriptures of the Bible, which is the word of God, written by holy men chosen of God. And, they wrote as they were moved by the Holy Spirit. (II Peter 1:20-21, II Timothy 3:16) The gospel has power, for it is the word of God – The Word of God is living and is quicker than any two-edged sword, sharp and powerful piercing even to the dividing asunder of soul and spirit, and of the joints and marrow, and is a discerner of the thoughts and intents of the heart. (Hebrews 4:12, 13; Romans 1:16; Genesis 1:1,3; Psalms 107:20; Job 26:7, Job 38:35) Now faith is the substance of things hoped for, the evidence of things not seen. (Hebrews 11:1) Sarah, being ninety years old and Abraham, being a hundred years old (Genesis 17:17) but with God all things are possible (Luke 1:37). Jeremiah 32:17 we must be steadfast, unmoveable, always abounding in the work of the Lord, knowing that our work in the Lord is not in vain (I Corinthians 15:58). We must not waver or be unstable in our faith in the Lord. It is essential that we hold fast to our faith in God; billows may roar, waves dash, the winds may blow; clouds in the sky, but Jesus will hold fast if we faint not. (James 1:5-8; John 14:6; John 20:24-31; Daniel 3:01-27; Daniel 6:10-28; Genesis 22:1-18; Genesis 5:22-24; Hebrews 11:1-6; John 17:20) If we believe in God, Christ, and the Holy Spirit, we will obey God. We will also trust God completely. We will love God and our fellow man; we will also yield ourselves completely to the guidance and teaching of the Holy Spirit, which is the working power of god, the third person in the trinity of God...God the Father of our Lord and Savior, Jesus Christ, the only begotten of Jehovah God and the Holy Spirit, the Comforter, who indwells in the saints of God. (Genesis 1:1-3; John 1:1, 12, 17; Luke 1:26-34-55; Matthew 1:25; John 16:33; Ephesians 2:14-22; Romans 5:1-21)

Faith is boundless (John 2:21-27). Faith is great (Matthew 8:10). Faith is holy (Jude 1:20). Faith is humble (Luke 7:6). Faith is mutual (Romans 1:12). Faith is perfect (James 1:22-27). Faith is precious (II Peter 1:1). Faith is united (Mark 2:5). Faith is small (Matthew 17:20). The fruits of faith...the remission of sins or the forgiveness of sin. (Acts 10:43-46; Acts 2:16,18; Acts 13:16-52) Freedom from condemnation. (John 3:16, 18) Justification. (Acts 13:39) Salvation. (Mark 16:20) Sanctification. (Acts 15:9) Freedom from spiritual death. (John 2:25-26) Spiritual light. (John 20:31) Eternal life. (John 3:16) Access to God. (Ephesians 3:12) Adoption. (John 1:12) Edification. (I Timothy 1:4) Preservation. (John 10:26-29) Inheritance. (??? 26-18) Peace and rest. (Romans 5:2-21) We are to live by faith. (Romans 1:17) Walk by faith. (Romans 4:12, 25; II Corinthians 5:7) Pray by faith. (Matthew 21:22; Mark 2:22-24; John 2:40-46) Overcome the world by faith. (I John 2:13-17; John 16:33; John 17:20) Example by faith. (Mark 10:46, 52) When we have true faith in God, we will obey God, know the gospel, and obey the gospel. We will also share the good news of the gospel with others in love. We must love the Lord our God with all our heart, and with all our soul, and with all our mind. This is the first and great commandment. And, the second is like unto it: thou shalt love thy neighbor as thyself. (Matthew 22:37-39) There are many other scriptures which I would like to share with each of you, but unfortunately, the time allowed will not permit me to do so. However, I shall endeavor to continue to associate faith and stewardship. Of course, they go hand in hand, and so, one without the other is dead. (James 2:1-26)

Let's take a closer look at the word "stewardship". What is the scientific of stewardship? Stewardship is trust granted for profitable use or management of entrusted duties; a guardian or overseer. (Genesis 43:19; Genesis 44:1; Matthew 20:8; I Peter 4:10-19; Acts 5:29; I Peter 5:1-4) Ministers of God or pastors are stewards of the household of God. They don't own the church or the congregation. They are placed in these positions as servants of God, to feed the flock of God, not by force, nor for money, but with a ready mind; neither as being lords over God's heritage but being examples to the flock. Because the Lord is the shepherd of the flock, which is the church of God and Christ. (I Thessalonians 1:1) The church is the body of Christ. Christ is the head of the church. (Colossians 1:18-24; Ephesians 1:21, 23) The church belongs to Christ because He gave His life and shed His blood on Calvary for His church. We are merely servants in the household of God, working for the glory of God. (I Corinthians 10:31, Ephesians 2:19, 22) We find this in the book of James, chapter two, verses thirteen through twenty-six. And, so, because of our faith in God, we become faithful workers or good stewards in God's kingdom, doing all of the things which God has told us to do. And, that is to be doers of the word and not hearers only, deceiving your own selves. (James 1:22-27; Luke 16:1-17) Trust in the Lord with all your heart and lean not unto your own understanding; in all your ways, acknowledge Him and He will direct your paths.

SYLLABUS / COURSE OUTLINE

REV. DR. FRANCES McINTYRE INSTRUCTOR

DESCRIPTION: SPIRITUAL GIFTS

COURSE OUTLINE

These courses are designed for people who have a sincere desire to know and identify as well as to exercise their spiritual gifts given to us by God. For edification and for the comfort of the body of Christ, which is the church of God and Christ (I Corinthians 1:2, Ephesians 1:2 & 3:23) governed by the Holy Spirit (I Corinthians 12:1-31 & 14:1-40).

GOALS / OBJECTIVES

1. To teach students in a comprehensive manner as we are led by the Holy Spirit how to identify their spiritual gifts.
2. To share scriptural information pertaining to spiritual gifts.
3. To employ and insure that the information is scriptural and biblical.
4. To promote and encourage students to know, identify, and to use their spiritual gifts for the edification and comfort of the church, which is the body of Christ. (Ephesians 1:22-23)
5. To teach them how to rely completely on the Holy Spirit when they use their spiritual gifts.

6. To teach them that they must ask God for wisdom, knowledge, and understanding when using or exercising their spiritual gifts.

7. To emphasize because they are spiritual gifts, that they must be used for the glory of God.

8. To help students to understand that hey must not let their spiritual gifts lie dormant.

9. To encourage students to pray and ask God to reveal to them what their spiritual gifts are. (Every born-again Christian has gifts.)

10. To help them to understand that only God knows what our spiritual gifts are.

STUDENTS OBJECTIVES

1. To teach students to actively and prayerfully seek to know and to identify their spiritual gifts.

2. To become actively involved in using their spiritual gifts for the glory of God!

3. To make sure that they spend quality time in prayer to God and be sure to read the word of God on a daily basis as well as to meditate on the word day and night. (Psalms 1:2)

4. To ask God daily for wisdom, knowledge, understanding, strength, and to know the will of God for our lives and to do the will of God for His glory!

5. To encourage them to have complete faith in God. (Hebrews 1:1-6)

6. To know that God hears our prayers and will answer our prayers!

7. To emphasize that it is imperative that we show Godly love and concern for others, not just in words but in deeds also.

8. To know God and His word and to make Him known to others as we are guided by the Holy Spirit!

9. To love God with all our heart, soul, mind, and strength, and to love others as we love ourselves.

10. To seek first the kingdom of God and his righteousness and these things will be added unto us.

11. To trust in the Lord with all our heat, and lean not upon our own understanding but in all of our ways acknowledge God and He will direct our path!

This teaching session is designed to share some of the spiritual gifts given to Christians by God.

What are spiritual gifts? Answer: Spiritual gifts are given to Christians by God, during conversion, when we hear the word of God and believe the word of God and confess our sins, when we believe that Jesus Christ is the son of God and that He died for our sins. But, He rose again on the third day with all power in heaven and in earth in His hands. We must ask God to forgive us for our sins and accept Jesus Christ as our savior and Lord of our life. We must know Christ and obey Him and it is most necessary that we follow His example and lifestyle. (Mark 1:17-18, Matthew 19:27-30, Galatians 5:16)

SOME OF THE SPIRITUAL GIFTS ARE...

1. LIFE: Because life is a gift from God!! (Job 33:4) The spirit of God has made me and the breath of the Almighty has given me life!

2. LOVE: For God so loved the world that He gave His only begotten son that whosoever believes in Him shall not perish but have everlasting life! John 3:16

3. WISDOM: For the Lord gives wisdom. Out of His mouth comes knowledge and understanding. (Proverbs 2:6)

4. KNOWLEDGE: He that chastises the heathen, shall he not correct; he that teaches man knowledge, shall he not know? (Psalms 94:10)

5. UNDERSTANDING: Behold I have done according to your words Lo, I have given you a wise and understanding heart, so that there was none like you before, neither after you shall any arise like unto you. (I Kings 3:12)

6. FAITH: For by grace are you saved through faith and not of yourselves, it is the gift of God. (Ephesians 2:8, Hebrews 1:1-6)

7. HEALING: The source of healing comes from God! So, Abraham prayed unto God and God healed Abimelech and his wife and his maidservants and they bare children.

8. PREACHING: Preaching is ordained of God. And as you go, preach, saying the kingdom of God is at hand. (Matthew 10:7, John 15-16??)

9. TEACHING: Teaching is ordained of God. Jesus came and spake unto them saying all power is given unto me in heaven and in earth. Go you therefore and teach all nations baptizing them in the name of the father and of the son and of the Holy Spirit, teaching them to observe all things whatsoever I

have commanded you and lo, I am with you always, even unto the end of the world. Amen.

10. GIFT OF TONGUES: Speaking in tongues is not an earthly language nor a natural language but it is a spiritual language given to believers or Christians. (For he that speaks in an unknown tongue speaks not unto men but unto God. For no man understands him. Howbeit in the Spirit he speaks mysteries). (I Corinthians 14:15)

11. INTERPRETATION OF TONGUES: If any man speak in an unknown tongue, let it be by two or at the most by three and that by course and let one interpret but if there be no interpreter let him keep silence in the church and let him speak to himself and to God. (I Corinthians 14:28)

12. MIRACLES: Miracles can only be done by and through the power of God!

The same came to Jesus by night and said unto him, rabbi, we know that you are a teacher from God for no man can do these miracles that you do except God be with him.

13. DISCERNING OF SPRITS: Discerning of spirits can only be done through the power of God!

But you have an unction from the Holy One and you know all things. (I John 2:20)

14. MERCY: Mercy is God's great compassion and love.

It is of the Lord's mercies that we are not consumed because His compassion fails not. They are new every morning. Great is thy faithfulness. (Lamentations 3:22-23)

15. GIVING: Giving or donate implies a free contribution, that your alms may be in secret and your Father which sees in secret shall reward you openly. (Matthew 6:4)

16. GOVERNING OR GOVERNMENT: Governing is recognized leadership given by God!

I have raised him up in righteousness and I will direct all his ways; he shall build my city and shall let go my captives not for price nor reward saith the Lord of hosts. (Isaiah 45:13)

COURSE REQUIREMENTS

Students are encouraged to actively participate in all class discussions, to express orally, in written compositions concerning the contents of class subject matter. Punctuality and regular attendance is essential and strongly required.

TEXT BOOKS

The Holy Bible and a Dictionary

Poems And Prayers

The Sky

Why does the sky appear so close, but still so far away?
No matter where you go, the sky is near as before.
Scientists say that the sky is light years away,
But the question still remains..
Why does the sky appear so near and yet is so very far away?
No matter where I roam or go in the universe,
The sky remains the same distance from every point or place.
From one starting point or place to the end,
The sky remains the same distance
Who can explain this mystery?
For God alone knows the distance, for it is God who
Created and made the sky!

Love

What is love? God is love. I John 4:8-16. Love is life because God is life. John 14:6, John 11:25. What is love; love is giving and love is loving without qualifications. Love is genuine consolation in time of sorrow; love is helping some one find a way. Love is praying for those who spitefully use you. Love is sharing with those in need. Love is witnessing for Christ. Love is praying and obeying God. Love is being truthful and sincere. Love is implementing the teaching of Christ. Love is forgiving. Love is thinking pure thoughts. Philippians 4:8. Love is verbal gratitude to God for His multitude of blessings. Love is taking inventory and appreciation for God's vast and beautiful creation. Love is the ultimate. Love is comforting those in need. Love is the blessings of God.

Love is caring. Love is being concerned for the welfare of others. Love is doing the will of God. Love is everything that's good. Love is pure. Love is honesty and fairness in every situation. Love is daily giving thanks and praise to Jehovah and acknowledging Him in all things. For God so loved the world that He gave His only begotten son that whosoever believeth in Him shall not perish, but have everlasting life, John 3:16.

REV. DR. FRANCES MCINTYRE

A Prayer of Praise and Thanksgiving

(4-29-96, approximately 9:15am)

Dear Heavenly Father, Father of our Lord and Savior, Jesus Christ. I come to you in the name of Jesus Christ and I thank you for your greatness and your greatness is truly unsearchable and cannot be measured. You are most worthy of all praise and thanksgiving. Because you love us with an everlasting love, and your mercy endures forever, to all generations. Your amazing grace is sufficient for any and every situation. And, your power reaches above the heavens and far beneath the earth. For, it is because of and by your mighty power, Jehovah God, you who is the beginning and the ending, the almighty God and the creator who created all things in heaven and in earth by your power!

It is and was you, God Almighty, who in the beginning, created all things and everything! Genesis 1:3 says: And God said let there be light and there was light! And, so, it is the truth that light came into existence by the power of your word. It was and is you, Heavenly Father, Jehovah God Almighty, who is the beginning and the ending. Almighty God, you are the first and the last! You know the ending at the beginning. It is and was you who stretched out the north over the empty place and hang the earth upon nothing. It was you in the beginning by your eternal power who spoke and said let there be light and there was light. And, that light still exists and will always exist. For you are the light of the world. You made and created the light by the power of your word! For you created everything and all things by the power of your eternal word! You created the things that are visible and invisible.

It is the truth that you are in complete control of everything and all things. Because before you, there was no god formed, neither shall there be after. Isaiah 43:10 says you are my witnesses saith the Lord and my servants whom I have chosen; that you may know and believe me and understand that I am He: before me there was no god formed, neither shall there be after me. For from everlasting to everlasting, you are God. Thank you for your greatness, goodness, blessings, miracles, protection, lovingkindness, guidance, teaching, and for your eternal healing power and much, much more. Your wonderful blessings are far too numerous to numerically count. For they are more than the grains of sand beside the sea shore. Help us to use these gifts and blessings wisely which you give to us so lovingly and generously moment by moment. And, they are precious gifts and blessings because we cannot work or pay for them. Because every thing was and is made by you. Even we, as human beings, are created and made by you, Heavenly Father. We are a part of your creation. Psalms 24:1 says the earth is the Lord's and the fullness thereof; the world and they that live in the earth. And, everything belongs to you.

It is the truth that you, God, are the source of all power. You, Heavenly Father, are in complete control of everything. Help us to praise you, thank you, love you, serve you, and obey you only. For you are all-powerful. You know everything and you are everywhere all the time at the same time. We move, live, and have our being because of you. We exist because of you. Heavenly Father, Lord God Almighty, teach us your word and teach us how to pray. Help us to understand your word and guide us as we share your Holy Word with others as we are guided by your Holy Spirit. Help us to follow the example of Jesus Christ, who is the one and only role model that we all must follow in order to be righteous in everything we do and say. Lord, we love you. We praise you. We adore you, and we thank you for all of your blessings in Jesus' name. Amen.

Prayer
(6-14-2000)

Dear Heavenly Father, Jehovah God Almighty, you who are the creator of all things in heaven and in the earth. I thank you for Jesus Christ our Lord and Savior. Thank you for your Holy Spirit who is our comforter, guide and our teacher, whom you have sent to live in your people, the believers; who have heard and read your Holy Word, and have and do believe that you are the one and only true God! Because you are the beginning and the ending. You are the first and the last, the Alpha and the Omega. You are the Almighty God of heaven and earth. Because you are the source of all power! You are everywhere all the time at the same time. You know all things and everything! For you are the creator of all things visible and invisible. You call those things that be not as though they were. For from everlasting to everlasting, you alone are God! Besides you, there is no god formed and neither shall there be after. For you alone are God! Bless your holy and righteous name forever and ever. Lord, we love you. We thank you. Lord God, we praise you. Alleluia! Alleluia! Alleluia! Thank you Jesus! Thank you Holy Spirit! Alleluia! Alleluia! Alleluia! Thank you God Almighty in Jesus' name, for your many blessings, for healing; for your wonderful miracles, protection, gifts, for eternal life through Jesus Christ, our Lord and Savior; for your Holy Spirit, who is our comforter, and for all your wonderful blessings, which you bestow upon us daily, moment by moment.

Help us to praise you with a pure heart. Please, help us to love you as you have directed us according to your holy word. Holy heavenly father, please, help us to obey and serve you only! Lord God Almighty, help us to first seek your kingdom and your righteousness, and all other things will be added unto us. Help us to trust in you with all our heart and lean not unto our own understanding, but in all our ways, acknowledge you, and you will direct our paths. Help us to do those things which YOU have told us to do for your glory. You will keep him in perfect peace whose mind is stayed on you because he trusts in you. Trust in the Lord Jehovah for in the Lord Jehovah is everlasting strength. Help us to remember to pray and read your Holy word everyday as we are guided by your Holy Spirit. Help us also to share your word with others as we are guided by your Holy Spirit.

Heavenly Father, please direct us in our witnessing as we share with others. Please direct and guide us in every thing we do and say. Lord God, Almighty, save all of my children and their children as well as their husbands and wives as well as my brothers and sisters and their families. I pray that you will save, bless, heal, deliver, teach, guide, and protect from all harm, hurt, and from all evil, including all people among all nations throughout the universe or world, according to your will and for your glory. I pray that you will save, heal, teach, guide, protect, comfort, and give peace to all people among all nations, throughout the whole world; men, women, boys, girls, infants, young and old, according to your Holy will in Jesus' name. I pray and ask. Praise your holy name forever and ever. Amen.

Prayer
(10-01-2001)

Dear Heavenly Father, you alone are God and beside you there is no god. Before you, there was no god formed, neither shall there be after. For, from everlasting to everlasting, you alone are God. You are the ending and the beginning. You are the first and the last. You are the source of all power! You are the one and only creator! For you created the heaven and the earth and everything that is in the heaven and everything that is in the earth. You created the things that are visible and things that are invisible. Lord God Almighty, help us to love you with all our heart, with all our soul, with all our mind, with all our strength, and help us to love others as we love ourselves. Teach us your word and teach us how to pray. Help us to obey you and your word. Thank you for your blessings, protection, love, and answered prayers. In Jesus' name. Amen.

About the Author

Dr. McIntyre is a servant of the most high God! The Creator who is the source of all power. She is an alumna of DePaul University, she received a Th.D from the theological seminary in Jerusalem, a Master's degree of Sociology, teaching certificate from the Environmental Department of Education, completion certificates from the National Baptist Publishing Board, Progressive National Baptist Convention Inc., National Council of Churches of Christ in the USA., Participatory certificates from police workshops, hospital chaplain and prison ministries, approved by the American Council of Education. Served as Dean of Student and faculty member for the Chicago Baptist Institute, Board of Trustee, Judge of Election, and is a civic and community activist.

Printed in the United Kingdom
by Lightning Source UK Ltd.
108892UKS00002B/256